LAUNCHING SHEEP

&

Other Stories from the Intersection of History and Nonsense

LAUNCHING SHEEP

&

Other Stories from the Intersection of History and Nonsense

Sarah Angleton

Bright Button Press · St Louis

Published by Bright Button Press
Copyright © 2017 Sarah Angleton

Cover Design by Steven Varble

Cover Photo by Karen Anderson Designs, Inc.

Costume Design by Laurabeth Allyn

ISBN-13 978-09987085318

Library of Congress Control Number: 2017904499

To Paul and Boys

Acknowledgements

Five years ago, my friend Samuel Hall told me that every writer needs a blog. Whether that's true or not, I am grateful to him for his encouragement because it's been a great five years. At the time I didn't imagine I would ever collect some of these scraps of life and history into a book, and I certainly owe thanks to many people for inspiring this project and helping to make it happen. Thank you to Carol Angleton for her unwavering enthusiasm. Thank you also to Karen Anderson, Laurabeth Allyn, and Steven Varble for taking my ridiculous ideas and making them beautiful. Also, thank you to Margo Dill, the best editor a girl could ask for and without whom, I'm pretty sure I would never, ever put a comma, in, the right, place; and don't even get me started on semi-colons. To my parents who never cease to cheer me on, and have even gone so far as to include a reference to my blog in their annual Christmas letters, I am so grateful for their support. I am very thankful to my husband, my first reader who is always ready with a title suggestion, and to my sons who over the years have been so willing to see their antics splashed across many of these posts. And most of all, I want to thank the many readers who have joined in the fun along the way, commenting and sharing and laughing with (and maybe at) me, and the crazy supportive Wordpress community of bloggers. If I could thank each one individually I would, but that would require a separate book.

Contents

Introduction

The Father of History's Pants Are on Fire

Sometime around 600 BC, Corinth's Periander the Tyrant (who was generally thought to be to a pretty okay guy) went for a stroll along the beach and came upon a pretty big surprise. What he found was a waterlogged musician in full musicians' garb with a wild story to tell.

Arion of Methymna was a uniquely gifted singer who could play a mean lyre. His talents were sought far and wide. In fact, Arion had been returning to Corinth from a tour in Italy, where he'd made a fat lot of cash, when calamity fell upon him.

Because unbeknownst to him, he was traveling with a crew of low-down, good-for-nothing Corinthians who took a shine to his fat lot of cash. The crew demanded the money and offered Arion a choice. He could either kill himself and expect a respectful land burial, or he could let them throw him into the sea.

The musician suggested a third option. He offered to put on his fine musicians' clothing and sing a song for them all, before he took his own life. The crew accepted the offer of the free concert, and Arion performed his heart out. Then he threw himself into the sea.

And that would probably have been the end of Arion of Mathymna, if it hadn't been for one heroic dolphin that happened by just in time to offer him a lift back to Corinth.

As you might imagine, Periander wasn't immediately convinced of the veracity of this tale, but clearly the musician had been through some ordeal, so he took Arion home and got him all cleaned up, placing him under guard, lest he hurt himself or someone else.

Then the ship full of low-down, good-for-nothing Corinthians with a new fat lot of cash, pulled into the harbor. Periander sent word to them, asking them what had become of his friend the musician, to which the scoundrels replied that as far as they knew Arion was safe and sound in Italy.

It was then that Arion presented himself to them in his full musicians' attire (hopefully dry-cleaned since his dolphin encounter), and they were amazed. Probably also a little concerned that they were going to spend a long time in Corinthian prison.

We know the tale of Arion and the dolphin because it was one of many included in *The Histories*, published by the Greek writer Herodotus sometime around 425 BC. The large work (later divided into nine books) was breaking new ground. It represented the first time a writer had taken a methodical, studious approach to researching and writing about the events of the past.

Herodotus called it *The Histories* because in Greek, the word refers to inquiries, a good description of the well-traveled scholar's approach to his subject. We call our inquiries into the past "history" because of the "father of history," Herodotus, the very first man to diligently study the past, and then kind of make it up as he goes.

Because even though Herodotus stated that his purpose for writing the work, which centered on the Greco-Persian Wars, was to ensure that "the deeds of men not be erased by time," he wasn't strictly concerned about the facts surrounding those deeds of men.

There is no question among historians that *The Histories* offer us some of the most detailed and reliable information of the ancient world we have and that Herodotus was a generally okay guy. But it can sometimes be problematic that with the same authority, the father of history also relays hearsay, exaggerations, and stories about European cyclopes and musician-rescuing dolphins. In other words, Herodotus was fascinated not just by history, but also by the way it was experienced, remembered, and shared.

He received a lot of criticism for this from his contemporaries. The Athenian historian Thucydides, whose *History of the Peloponnesian War* written just a few years later made him the father of scientific history (because he made the choice not to write about daring dolphin rescues), complained that Herodotus was a liar, liar, pants on fire because he included fables as history just to liven things up a bit.

And whether that was a fair criticism or not, Herodotus did include fables and hearsay in his writing. Today's historians are still debating just how reliable *The Histories* really are, and the father of history is still occasionally referred to as the father of lies. His work can feel a little like reading a Wikipedia article that's been contributed to by a lot of folks that all sound pretty knowledgeable, but don't actually reference any reliable sources.

Or maybe it's like reading the blog of a *practical historian*, who approaches history from the viewpoint of a storyteller, looking for the interesting bits about European cyclopes and daring dolphin rescues. She does try to share factual information most of the time; but while she often refers to a primary source, she's also just as likely to depend too heavily on that Wikipedia article contributed to by people who sound pretty knowledgeable, but don't bother to reference any reliable sources.

Don't get me wrong. I'm grateful for the diligent historians out there in the Thucydides camp, scientifically combing through source material, seeking confirmation of their careful assumptions, and making every attempt to remove bias from their work as much as humanly possible. They're really the ones doing the hard work of ensuring that the deeds of men don't get erased by time.

But I think Herodotus and I could have hung out. I think there's power to viewing fact through the lens of interpretation. I like his style. I admit, I have been known to throw the occasional bit of hearsay or exaggeration in with my facts because I'm fascinated by the way history has been and is experienced, remembered, and shared. I love that experiences from even thousands of years ago can in some ways sound so familiar within the context of my own life and experiences today.

For the last five years I've been exploring history from that perspective in a weekly blog post on a little Wordpress site I chose to call *The Practical Historian: Your Guide to Practically True History*. During that time I've written novels, my family has moved halfway across the country, we've gotten a dog, and we've traveled, laughed and grown. A lot of that has served as my lens, and it shows up on the blog and in this book as well.

I'll let the professional historians sort out the dates and details and important stuff. I'll keep my focus on stories about daring dolphin rescues, the lunacy of voluntary jogging, exceptionally bad hairdos, probably ill-conceived stunts, and even worse inventions.

If you're unfamiliar with the blog, you can find it at www.sarah-angleton.com, where in the midst of constructing far more serious works of historical fiction, I'm still plugging away, sharing a mix of fun historical facts and nonsense while wearing pants that might occasionally be on fire.

Those That Do Not Study History are Doomed to Fail the Class

Proudly displayed on the wall of the social studies department office in my high school was a poster with the words (in fancy script, indicating both grave importance and light-hearted fun all in one colorful design): "Those who fail to learn from history are doomed to repeat it." I took this as the dire warning it was meant to be…I was probably going to fail my history classes and be forever trapped by the mistakes of blind ignorance.

Of course at the time, I was a teenager and already swimming in the mistakes of blind ignorance. Desperate to graduate from high school, I wanted only to move on with my life to a college campus, where they were much more blasé about learning, and I could carefully avoid any further exposure to this subject we call history.

And avoid it I did. I received a bachelor of science degree in four years from a respected state funded institute of higher learning while only taking one class from the history department. The subject was, in fact, something like

Contemporary American Religious Thought, which I suppose had as much to do with history as did the rest of my classes.

Against all odds, though, I now find myself (a thirty-something wife, mom, writer) fascinated by history. A few things, I think, contributed to this: 1. I went back to school to get a master's degree in the remarkably practical field of literature, 2. I married a guy who likes to watch the History Channel (when someone makes a mini series from my blog, he's promised to watch), and 3. I learned to Google.

My writing has recently taken me (purely by accident) into the realm of historical fiction. I am nearly finished with my first novel (meaning that I have a completed manuscript which I think is great, and I'm just waiting now for a carefully selected group of readers to tell me it's not). In reflecting on the experience, I marvel at how far I have come as a person, from the girl who read that (motivational?) poster all those years ago to a serious student of the past committed to thorough research. That's right, I Googled the quote.

Here's what I found:

No one really seems to know who said it. The most adamant (even a little irrationally angry if you ask me) sources insist that it is misquoted from Spanish-American philosopher George Santayana, who wrote in a couple of his books: "Those who cannot remember the past are condemned to repeat it." Okay, I'll buy that, but it's also attributed (in various forms) to Edmund Burke, Winston Churchill, Benjamin Franklin, Confucius, and Lemony Snicket. One source even had the nerve to suggest that Aristotle may have said it, but boy did that guy get what was coming to him in the court of Internet opinion!

I think what this illustrates is that history is far more fluid than we'd like to believe. As we recall the dates and events from our history books, it's important to keep in mind that a handful of verifiably true statements come together to tell a story. Trouble is each of us will tell the story a little bit differently. As a teenager, and into my early twenties, I found that concept difficult to grasp and so I avoided the problem. Then I began to seriously study the art of storytelling. What I found was that the literature of a time period (particularly that which was widely read, though to a lesser extent also that which has been deemed by scholars to be representative of the period) gives us a great glimpse into history. Even literature that does not directly comment upon its age allows us to reflect, for a time, upon the mindset and experiences of the people who wrote, presumably for an audience that they at least thought they understood.

This gets even trickier when we start thinking about historical fiction. As a writer of such, I must be ever mindful that I am borrowing the era and should make every effort to treat it with respect. I must also realize that no matter what lens I attempt to use in order to make a particular time and place accessible to my reader, the truth is I am a 21st-century writer communicating with a 21st-century audience and so any version of history I tell will always be colored by 21st-century sensibilities. And what I've decided is that not only is this unavoidable, but it is also perfectly okay because no era (even the contemporary one) exists in a vacuum. This is, of course, the point of that oh-so-famous quote about the importance of learning about and from history.

History builds upon itself. One cannot tell a story or make a memorable statement without the influences of the past. Did Winston Churchill say, "Those that fail to learn history are doomed to repeat it?" He probably did. Did he adapt it from George Santayana, who borrowed it from Benjamin Franklin, who got it from Edmund Burke, who snatched it from Confucius? Perhaps Confucius had a time machine and enjoyed the clever wit of Lemony Snicket, though frankly I find it more likely Snicket read it in a fortune cookie. I don't know, but doesn't that make a great story?

May 16, 2012

"An Arbitrary, Ridiculous Thing"

My youngest son has had an unfortunate habit since the time he was very little. He innocently points with his middle finger. We've tried (while carefully hiding our snickers behind our hands) to break him of it with gentle reminders that pointer finger is for pointing, but even at nearly 5, he sometimes reverts to it. Now we also remind him that it is a rude gesture and he is quick to correct himself.

But as he's getting bigger he's starting to get more contemplative and wants to know not just how the world works, but also why things are the way they are. Enter the difficult questions. I'm not talking about the "What happens when I die" and "where do babies come from" questions that every parent dreads. Those questions, I think I am *mom enough* to handle. What gets me are the ones for which I genuinely do not know the answer. Like this one:

"Why is it rude to show my middle finger to someone?"

When "it just is" no longer satisfies, I am forced to do a little research to ask where and why this offensive gesture first popped up. Here's the story:

The setting is France in the year 1415 during the Battle of Agincourt (obviously, you all remember that one). The French soldiers got caught up in that oh-so-French tradition (as any Monty Python fan can attest) of mocking their English enemies. Specifically, they pompously informed the English bowmen that they would capture them all and cut off their middle and index fingers. Those being the fingers they used to pluck the strings on their bows, custom designed and crafted from the yew trees of their homeland, this was a creatively violent threat. Now I'm sure I don't need to tell you the outcome of the battle, but for those of you history-phobes (yes, it's a word) who might have temporarily forgotten, the battle didn't go as the French planned. When the fighting was over, the English bowmen proudly displayed their index and middle fingers and shouted, "We can still pluck yew!" At that point, what remained of the French army ran away groaning.

As a practical historian, I really can't ask for a better story than this, complete with punch line. The legend continues that over the years the two fingered gesture became the one-finger gesture we know today, and well, you can probably imagine what happened to the phrase.

But it's not likely true (I know. I can't help feeling a little sad, too). Actually the gesture dates back to long before 1415. It shows up as far back as Ancient Greece, and the Romans apparently loved it so much they had a special name for it, the *digitus impudicus* (roughly translated as the finger with which one plucks yew). Humans have been playing around with this one obscene gesture literally for millennia.

But that doesn't answer the question of why it is considered so rude. I think we can learn the most by examining when it's used. At its core, "flying the bird" is a display of aggression in a situation when actual aggression is either impossible or ill-advised. It has become a universal symbol for "Boy, am I mad at you!"

Unfortunately, it has become so ubiquitous, its applications so varied, that it can also mean such things as: "I'm sure I'm not the first person to let you know what a terrible driver you are, but just in case…," "Why yes, officer, I am anxious to go to prison," "I have a political statement to make, but truth be told, I'm not all that articulate," and "It turns out I don't actually have anything for you in my pocket after all."

I think, then, it's best if we turn to an expert to clear this up for us, and by *expert*, I mean Jerry Seinfeld. Of the aforementioned gesture, Seinfeld says:

"It seems like such an arbitrary, ridiculous thing ...Someone shows it to me and I'm supposed to feel bad...I mean, you could give someone the toe, really, couldn't you? I would feel worse if I got the toe...'cause it's not easy to give someone the toe, you've gotta get the shoe off, the sock off, and drive, get it up and...'look at that toe, buddy.' I mean that's really insulting to get the toe, isn't it?"

Just maybe, then, the offensiveness of today's middle finger gesture is really about a lack of creativity. That's an answer I can give my son. The next time he asks me why the middle finger is rude my response may go something like this:

People put up their middle fingers to express frustration with others, and while it's okay to be frustrated, it is always rude to disregard people as not worth our best efforts. By displaying our middle fingers, we are blatantly copying off of our ancestors from thousands of years ago and are thus participating in unimaginative communication. We owe our fellow humans more than that, don't you think?

May 23, 2012

Why Does the Sun REALLY Not Shine?

Last Sunday, a dragon ate the sun. At least I think it did. I was planning to watch an annular eclipse (when the moon passes in front of the sun, leaving only a perfect ring of fire for a time). This super cool astronomical event was visible throughout much of the Western United States, including my house, where it was supposed to occur around 4:00 Pacific Time. We were ready for it, too. We'd done the research and explained to our boys the danger of staring directly at the sun (for days our littlest refused to look anywhere but directly at his feet whenever he went outside).

My husband dug out the rarely used binoculars and rigged up a fancy contraption using a stepladder, some duct tape, and a piece of white poster board, so that we could see a shadow of the glorious event. After much anticipation, Sunday finally arrived, and we remembered something very important: we live in Western Oregon, where it really isn't that rare to not see the sun. After over a week of clear, sunny skies, our eclipse was completely obscured by clouds.

Instead of a live shadow of an annular eclipse, we tuned in to a webcast from the National Park Service—live from New Mexico—where, thankfully, there wasn't a cloud in the sky. So, via the miracle of the Internet, we got to see (drumroll, please) part of a white circle against a dark background. The less than spectacular image was a result of the special light filters on the camera lens because apparently, it really is dangerous to look directly at the sun.

Now, I'm not trying to downplay the eclipse. It really is a cool thing if you think about it, even if it is frightening and dangerous to directly observe. In fact, people have been fascinated by eclipses for thousands of years. The ancient Egyptians observed eclipses at least 4500 years ago, the Chinese, at least 4000 years ago.

And why not? If the sun occasionally vanishes, and the moon sometimes turns blood red, I think it might be worth taking note. As one might expect, there are lots of mythological explanations for eclipses. Almost all express a great deal of fear (leading me to believe that if the sun really were to vanish from the sky, it might be bad), and many involve a large celestial animal of some sort actually eating the sun, my favorite of which is that of Ancient China in which a dragon is responsible.

The Chinese even had a practical solution to their dragon problem because (as everyone knows) dragons are afraid of loud noises. So when the large celestial dragon showed up to eat the sun, everyone simply made as much noise as they could, banging on drums or what have you, and the dragon went away. It worked! But here's the truly strange part: there is recorded evidence of Chinese sailors setting off cannon fire to scare away the eclipse dragon as recently as the 19th century, yet Chinese astronomers understood the real scientific cause of eclipses for sure by the year 20 BCE. So why did the myth persist?

I like to think it's because it's true, but then again most of what I know about the sun I learned from They Might Be Giants. On their 1993 EP, the band covered a song by Hy Zaret entitled "Why Does the Sun Shine?" (If you haven't heard it, you really should give it a listen). In this song, the band reveals all kinds of information about our sun, not the least of which is the fact that it is a "mass of incandescent gas." Trouble is scientists now tell us it's not. So in their more recent (2009) album *Here Comes Science*, the band performs a new song called "Why Does the Sun Really Shine?" in which they update the theory by explaining that "the sun is a miasma of incandescent plasma."

Maybe it is. I tend to believe that scientists more or less know what they're doing (at least until someone comes along and convinces the world they don't), but that doesn't change the fact that I like the first song better. It's catchier, more fun to sing. More importantly than that, it represents the collective scientific thoughts about the sun at the time it was written, and as such, it still has value, doesn't it? Maybe no longer as scientific theory, but perhaps as the history of scientific theory, which is really just a reflection of how we have experienced our universe over time.

So maybe the 19th century Chinese navy really did know what was what when they fired off the cannons to scare away the sun-eating dragon, but by acknowledging the mythological history, they celebrated the noble tradition of human imagination. I like that very much.

Though unspectacular in many ways, I admit to a few shivers of awe when that dark circular blob positioned itself directly in the center of the white circle on my computer screen. I may have even cheered out loud, though that's probably because deep down I was trying to scare away the dragon.

May 30, 2012

One Small Step for Livestock...

In 1830, an Italian pyrotechnician by the name of Claude Ruggieri announced a truly wondrous event. The latest in a long line of successful Ruggieri firework producers, Claude was particularly devoted to the study of rocketry and had begun, in as early as 1806, to successfully launch small rodents high into the atmosphere (frankly, it was about time someone got around to doing that). As others wasted their genius merely developing more effective weapons delivery systems, Claude Ruggieri proved to be a true pioneer when in 1830, he finally announced that he would, for the purposes of public demonstration of his company's rocket-making prowess, launch a sheep from the Champs de Mars in Paris, where he was living at the time.

As exciting as this may sound, it wasn't enough for one young man who eagerly volunteered to take the animal's place. Ruggieri accepted the gracious offer (much to the relief of the sheep), and the launch was re-advertised. Unfortunately, Paris authorities investigated, discovered that the volunteer was in fact an 11-year-old boy, and determined that though perfectly old enough to board the Hogwarts Express, 11 was perhaps not yet mature enough to display good judgment in regard to experimental rocketry. The launch did, however, go ahead as originally planned, and the once again greatly dismayed sheep was fired 600 feet into the air (not exactly suborbital, but not bad by 1830-sheep-launching standards) only to land gently by parachute, alive and instantly famous.

Though Ruggieri's success may not seem like a big deal now that we've been to the moon, roved Mars, and rely daily upon satellite technologies, his "combination [sheep launching] rocket" was pretty innovative. And while I can't say that his work formed an important basis for that which followed in the field of rocket science, his story does nicely illustrate the plucky can-do attitude that has plagued the field since it's earliest days when legendary Chinese official Wan Hoo attached rockets to his wicker chair in an attempt to launch himself to the moon (because he was never seen again, I think we can safely assume he made it).

So if we skip ahead a few years to the 1957 Russian launch of Sputnik, it's not hard to imagine that the excitement of that event may have led to some poor judgment on the part of the enthusiastic, though sadly under-qualified, masses. And a new industry was born.

In 1954, Robert Carlisle, a model airplane enthusiast, needed a model to use for demonstration purposes when he lectured on rocket-powered flight, and so he approached his brother Orville, a pyrotechnics expert, to help him design it. When Sputnik went up and the masses began their various dangerous experiments, the Carlisle brothers saw an opportunity. Using their newfound expertise, they developed a (relatively) safe model rocket engine. Through a series of business partnerships, their design became the backbone of the Estes Corporation, still a major supplier of model rocket equipment, to which many wives and mothers owe their gratitude.

This brings me to my weekend. Last Saturday, my husband and young sons held their first launches. Weeks of anticipating, assembling, painting, and planning culminated in a brief, but awesome, display of smoke and propulsion. All three rockets launched successfully and landed intact. Nothing (that wasn't supposed to) caught fire. and there were no injuries to children (or sheep).

Thank you to the Estes Corporation, to the Carlisle brothers, and to all those brave pioneers without whose guidance I am certain my boys (all three) would have launched something into the air anyway, and who knows what would have happened.

June 6, 2012

126 Simple Rules

By the end of this week, I will have shuttled my two sons to four different flag football practices. I should preface this by stating (and I really cannot stress this enough) that I am not a football person. I know, some women are huge fans of the sport and understand every tiny rule and obscure penalty on the books. Many may even know a thing or two about the players and can be described as genuinely dedicated fans whose loyalty is based on more than simply the color of their favorite team's uniforms. I'm just not one of those women. Of course, I am handy to have around when you're watching a game because I'll happily run to the kitchen for snacks.

And it's not that I *can't* understand the game (which I readily admit I don't). I am a reasonably intelligent person after all. It's really that, try as I might, I don't want to. It just seems to me that it may be the most unnecessarily complicated game in history. But then perhaps for some, it is this excessive complication which makes it (allegedly) so great.

The origin of the sport known the world over as American football (not to be confused with soccer with which, historically speaking, it probably has a great deal more in common than most hooligans would care to admit) has been traced, by people with far too much time on their hands, to the ancient Greek game of harpaston, a game with almost no rules at all. Here's all you need to know to play the game of harpaston:

1. If your team has the ball (may also sub a ripe melon, small animal, or severed head), you can score by running, kicking, or passing across the designated goal line.

2. If the other team has the ball, get it back.

There were no cumbersome boundary lines or regulations about numbers of players or lengths of fields. Harpaston was true sport in its finest potentially deadly form.

Little seems to have changed by the time the game shows up again, this time in 12th century England, where it was a game most often enjoyed during Carnival week (the week leading up to Lent). Two teams, again made up of an unspecified number of players, started in the market square and attempted to score goals in gates set up some distance from the square. Still, there were apparently no confining rules, which served to heighten the excitement, even encouraging merchants to close up shop and board their windows as mothers enthusiastically whisked their children indoors.

The playing of this classic Carnival week ball game continued relatively unmolested for over a century until one fateful February morning in 1314 when a gifted archer, (whose name is sadly lost to history) in loyal service to King Edward II, lost his bow-drawing (or yew plucking) fingers to the teeth of an over-eager duke on the opposing team. Edward was faced with a choice:

1. Ban the sport altogether (a move, which although popular amongst merchants and mothers, was not supported by the unruly hooligans who closely followed the progress of the sport and whose antics, frankly, made the king a little nervous).

2. Introduce a controversial no biting rule.

Edward chose to ban the sport, as a matter of general safety. In response to the king's great concern for the well-being of his subjects, the Carnival ball game hooligans set his car on fire (after flipping it over of course).

The sport resurged at various times through the years; but even the whisper of additional rules and safety regulations forever altered the course of football, which explains (just trust me on this) why in 1940, the sport of flag football began popping up on military bases in the US. Out of fear of the potential injuries caused by the now much more heavily regulated, though still brutal, game of football and an unwillingness to risk the able bodies of our men in uniform, a new version of the sport was born.

After the introduction of flags, the two parallel versions of the game developed more or less separately, though in many important ways are still roughly the same game. So just how many rules are there? According to one person on Answers.yahoo.com (whose moniker "Cu Tie" leaves little doubt in my mind that he or she is a football expert), there are approximately 11,500 rules listed in the 2011 NFL rule book. Of course human error being what it is, several less reputable people have sought to debunk this, claiming instead that there are in fact only 367. Either way, it's way more than two.

And I don't know about the average flag football league, but for the one in which my sons (who are entering Kindergarten and 2nd grade) participate, I count 126 separate rules, neatly listed on a parent handout (surprisingly "no biting" isn't included). And yes, we want the kids to be safe, to play fair, and to have a great time. I have to wonder, though, how many of these 126 rules will really be followed by a bunch of Kindergartners who still require daily reminders as to which side of their pants goes in the front. I would keep track, but honestly I'd rather run to the concession stand for a snack. I'd be happy to bring you something.

July 4, 2012

Upon the Seat of a Bicycle Built for Two

On our way out for a nice Sunday lunch this past weekend, my family and I spotted a pair of tandem bicycles cruising along the side of the road, an exciting event for my littlest, who had never seen one before. His response was something like: "Whoa! Those bikes are HUGE!"

We smiled (because you can't help but smile at a bicycle built for two) and drove on our way, only to discover that there were two more tandems up the road a bit, traveling in the same direction as the first. Weird. Next came a group of four. Then three. Around this time we started to think something significant might be happening. And sure enough, when I looked into it, I discovered that my fair city hosted the 27th Annual Northwest Tandem Bike Rally this past Sunday and Monday.

The Rally isn't a race, but rather a series of optional, mapped rides—some with bicycle maintenance support and some without— through a different Northwest city every year on 4th of July weekend. It's a family-friendly event, a time to share all of your tandem bike-related stories with others who get you.

At least that's what I gather. I'm not a tandem cyclist

myself, but (because I know you're curious) I learned a thing or two about them. The credit for the invention of the tandem bicycle is usually given to Dan Albone (arguably the father of the modern farm tractor, too, though that hardly seems as important), along with his partner Arthur James Wilson. The two patented their design in 1886.

You could say that the tandem bicycle was the sports car of the 19th century. Don't believe me? Here's what they were invented for:

1. Courting (the 19th century version of hooking up)

2. Speed.

The earliest designs, referred to most often as "courting bikes," had three or four wheels, instead of the two they have today; and the steering came from the back (what could possibly go wrong with that?). The idea was simple. A young fella who couldn't afford a carriage, but still wished to broaden his horizons beyond just the few marriageable girls next door, could hop on his bike and scour the countryside for the girl of his dreams. When he found her, he could put her on the front seat of his bicycle and show her the sights. If he was clever (and her name happened to be Daisy), he could even sing her a song about the experience.

But more than that, tandem bicycles were just as often designed for sport because with greater pedaling force and not that much more drag, tandems could (in the hands of good riders with good partnerships) reach greater speeds than could traditional bicycles. And of course if more riders=more power, then why stop at two? People (and by people here I pretty much mean guys) started designing bikes that could seat three, four, or even five riders. Then in 1897, the Oriental Bicycle Company took the logical next step when it produced a *ten-seat* tandem bicycle (probably not as practical as it sounds).

The speed of the more traditional two-seaters landed them a place in the 1906 Olympic Games, in which men competed in the 2000 meter tandem sprint. The event continued through 1972 when it was eliminated due to (probably not a shocker) excessive athlete injury.

Having never ridden on a tandem bike myself, I asked the only person I actually know who has ever ridden on one, about what it might be like. In the years 2010 and 2011, my sister biked a total of 2010 and 2011 miles respectively, mostly on a traditional road bike with a single seat, making her, in my book, a cycling expert (and maybe a tad bit of an overachiever). I recently discovered that a few of her logged miles occurred on the back of a tandem bicycle and she shared with me her impression of the experience.

What I gathered from her tale is that it's not really all that enjoyable. It turns out, true to the proverbial dog sled, if you're not the lead rider, the view never changes. The rider in the front of the modern tandem bike has all of the control *and* all of the view. The job of the rider in the back is simply to do his or her best to match the pedaling of the rider in the captain's seat. There's no pausing to look at scenery and there's no adjusting of the course. The rider in the back just has to trust that the one in control knows what he or she is doing.

And my sister brought up another important point as well. If you've ever done any *serious* cycling (like I have, but more on the "Tour de Donut" another time), then you may be familiar with a more delicate problem that plagues cyclists. As comfortable as bicycle seats may appear, it turns out, over long distances, they really can become relatively unpleasant on the rump.

Cyclists deal with this problem by wearing padded shorts and by taking the occasional opportunity to coast as they stretch, giving their sore bottoms a much needed break. Such a stretch is trickier on a tandem bike when the two cyclists have to carefully coordinate their movements. The lesson from this, I think, is that, as romantic as it may sound, a tandem bicycle ride may no longer be an ideal first date, as the topic of butt comfort will most likely come up and once it's out there, the odds of a second date probably decrease.

And it seems to me that this difficulty would increase exponentially with the number of riders on a single tandem bike, which may explain in part, why Oriental Bicycle Company's ten-seater (now housed by the Henry Ford Museum) was the last of its kind. But personally, I'm hoping it makes a comeback. Maybe in the 2016 Summer Olympics or at least as part of the 28th Annual Northwest Tandem Bike Rally.

Six Degrees of the Bacon Rebellion

As the early bird of the family, my youngest son rarely misses the chance to say a lengthy goodbye to my husband as he leaves for work every morning. This leads, sometimes, to some very funny little-kid send-offs (generally worthy of Christmas letters, status updates, and, yes, blog posts). A while ago, J. said to his dad, "Have a great day! Climb ladders; bring bacon." That he got from *The Incredibles*. Then he added, "Really, Daddy. Bring bacon. It's delicious!"

We laughed because of his obvious misunderstanding of the expression, but I recently learned that he wasn't really that far off. It turns out that "bringing home the bacon" may actually have nothing to do with breadwinning, but may instead derive from a tradition in a 12th century English town in which the church promised to award a side of bacon to any married man who could swear before God that he hadn't quarreled with his wife for a full calendar year.

But it's not my young son's insightful understanding of this common phrase that really surprises me. He is, after all, only repeating what he hears. But this is the same kid who recently watched the animated movie version of E.B. White's *Charlotte's Web;* and upon hearing the farmer at the end tell a crowd at the fair that his award winning pig Wilbur will live a long life, free from the butcher's knife, he asked, "But if they don't kill the pig, then how are all the people going to get bacon?"

The funny thing is the kid doesn't eat bacon or really any meat that isn't processed into a hotdog. Somehow, despite his disdain for all things meaty, an unwavering bacon obsession is leaking into his little brain.

Etymologically speaking, the word "bacon" refers to the back of an animal; though until the 17th century, it wasn't considered a specific cut of meat, but rather just as a term for any cut of pork. Today, bacon in the US mostly comes from pork bellies, and more than two billion pounds of it is produced annually. In some form, bacon shows up on history's radar as early as 1500 BC, and since that time has been a cheap and (if properly cured) easily stored meat for the masses in nearly every age. But no age has loved it quite as much as our own.

Sometime in, let's say, the last 20 years or so, bacon has taken on a new (and totally bizarre) life. No longer do we confine ourselves to eating bacon with our eggs at breakfast time, but we can now also purchase a variety of bacon related and/or bacon flavored products, including (though certainly not limited to):

Bacon soap, bacon-scented hand sanitizer, bacon flavored popcorn, gummy bacon, bacon lip balm, bacon toothpaste, bacon mints, bacon-scented air freshener, bacon gumballs, bacon lollipops, bacon soda (which is even more revolting than it sounds), bacon dental floss, and bacon jelly beans (though to be fair, the Bertie Bott's Corporation has been making those for over a century).

Presumably people are actually buying these products, which begs the question, WHY?

So here's my theory. Sometime in the 1980s the US began a steady slide into the health food craze. No longer was tofu a fringe food, the consumption of which attracted immediate ridicule. Suddenly, we became faced with a slew of health gurus touting the advantages of whole, natural, and nutritious foods, and somehow, we started to listen. While publicly many of us (practical historians included) say the healthier food of today is so much more flavorful (the polite way of saying, "This tastes an awful lot like grass,") what we really mean is: "We're hungry for bacon!"

This brings us to the Bacon Rebellion (not to be confused with the 1676 uprising led by Nathaniel Bacon against Virginia Governor William Berkeley and his policies regarding Native Americans, which I'm told is also of some historical importance). Bacon is the perfect poster food for the uprising against healthfulness, representative of everything doctors and dieticians tell us to avoid: salty, fatty, and delicious.

There are a million ways you can use it, too. Go ahead, name any food, and I bet that within six recipes, I can connect it to bacon. Because now thanks to good old-fashioned American ingenuity and pure stubbornness, we're even dipping it in chocolate!

That's right. Chocolate-coated bacon is sweeping the nation thanks to Marini's Candy in Santa Cruz, California, owned by brothers, Nick and Gino Marini, who claim to be the first to present the combination to the public. For their efforts, the Marini Brothers were featured on an episode of History Channel's *Modern Marvels*, a show dedicated to brilliant advances in technology (obviously this is a good programming fit).

So keep it up, all you health nuts out there. You're doing good work, and we all appreciate it. Some of us may even live longer because of your efforts. Just don't count bacon out because it has proven (with a fury unchallenged in the culinary world) that it remains the food the people still want to bring home.

I, for one, would not wish to quarrel with anyone who brings it to me covered in chocolate.

July 25, 2012

Life's a Piece (or Two) of Cake

In the last two weeks, I gained five pounds. I should clarify that this is not something I typically do. I am in fairly decent shape, and I take good care of my health more or less. Unfortunately recently, it's been less rather than more. The blame falls to birthday cake (well okay, to be fair, the blame rests with my complete and utter lack of will power, but let's just pretend it's the cake's fault).

July was a delicious month around our house. First, my husband had a birthday. Then my oldest son (a Christmastime baby) had a summer celebration for his birthday since it's so hard to celebrate with his friends during the holidays. Then my youngest son had a birthday, followed a few days later by a party with some of his little friends. All totaled, that's one ice cream cake, a traditional chocolate birthday cake decorated with multiple layers of frosting, and two separate batches of cupcakes.

I guess you could say I have been having my cake and eating it, too. But while that statement wouldn't exactly be untrue, it would be an inaccurate rendering of the famous "eating your cake" proverb.

The idiom first appears in the historical record in 1546 as

part of a catalogue of English proverbs collected by John Heyood, in which he asks: "Would you both eat your cake, and have your cake?" He actually spelled that quite differently; but as I generally speak modern English, I updated the quote a little, both for your convenience and so that you don't think me pretentious, like one of those people who would stop you mid-sentence to correct your grammar. (By the way, I am totally one of those people. I'm not proud of it.)

Apparently the phrase got plenty of use over the next couple hundred years as it shows up in satirist Jonathan Swift's 1738 "Polite Conversation" in which his mockery of the phrase indicates that it must have been a thoroughly overused cliché of his day. When the work was republished a few years later as "Tittle Tattle" (after Swift's death), the phrase had been reversed; thus, "She cannot eat her cake and have her cake" became "She cannot have her cake and eat her cake." After that (and I think if Swift were alive today, he would agree that I'm not exaggerating here), all hell broke loose. The reordered idiom not only seeped into common language, but by the 1940s, almost no one said it correctly anymore.

The original meaning of the phrase is, of course, about making a choice. If you have a cake and you choose to eat it, then you will no longer have a cake. You can't have it both ways. Cultures all over the world have developed sayings that express this same universal truth. In China, the saying goes that you cannot have a horse that both runs fast and consumes no feed. An Italian proverb goes something like: you can't have the barrel full and the wife drunk. And my personal favorite is from Russia: it's hard to have a seat on two chairs at once.

Of course the Russian idiom seems in some ways just as problematic as the reordered English proverb. If we consider that one both has a cake and eats it and if we assume that the phrase involves sequential activity (first you have a cake and then you eat it), then having just eaten an entire cake (or in my case multiple helpings of several cakes), you might require an additional chair to support your extra poundage.

I understand why people get a little picky about the proverb, though. If you think about it, to have a cake and eat it really has little to do with making a tough choice, and this is especially true when you have plenty of leftover cake and ample opportunity to grab a slice after the kids go to bed.

But the cake is finally gone, and there won't be another birthday in our house until October, giving me a good solid two months to count calories, exercise, and squeeze back into my skinny pants. It won't be much fun, but what can I expect? I ate my cake, and now I don't have my cake. And I will have to live with the consequences.

Eggs, Months, and Disciples

Recently, my husband and I celebrated our 12th wedding anniversary. Well okay, that's not exactly true. Twelve years have come and gone since we were married; but between kids' schedules, work schedules, and just plain fatigue, we've yet to really celebrate. I guess that's how it goes, though. As joyful as those years have been, it gets harder to party, and 12 doesn't really feel like a special number.

Perhaps that's why the earliest anniversary celebrations were reserved for years 25 and 50. The tradition, which most likely comes from the Middle Ages in the region that would eventually become Germany, was for a husband (or sometimes friends of the couple) to present the wife with a silver wreath in celebration of the 25th anniversary and a gold wreath for the 50th. It actually wasn't until the mid to late 1930s that more celebrations became common, and even then it was usually limited to the 1st, 10th, 20th, and 70th.

Traditionally these anniversaries are celebrated with gifts of increasing value to symbolize the increasing value of a commitment maintained over time. The paper (or freezer burned wedding cake) anniversary is up first. For the 10th, tin is the gift of choice (because nothing says love like a tin roof rusted). By the time you've been married 20 years, it's time to replace the wedding china (if any has survived the nesting stage); and if you are fortunate enough to see your 70th, the metal of choice is platinum (you spin me right 'round, baby, right 'round, like a platinum record, baby, right round, 'round, 'round).

And even though as time moves on and the divorce rate creeps up (in the US the average marriage that ends in divorce lasts between 7 and 8 years; the average overall is just 24 years) and couples become more likely to treat each anniversary as an achievement, I'm still not sure when we will get around to calling a babysitter and grabbing that romantic dinner for two. Maybe I'll just have to face the fact that some anniversaries seem more celebration worthy than others.

But before I do, I would like to make a case for year number 12.

First of all, great things come in twelves. Things like eggs, months, disciples, hours on the clock, signs of the zodiac, tribes of Israel, and drummers drumming. We regularly bake cookies, cupcakes, and muffins in multiples of 12. And 12 even has its own special title (a claim to fame shared by such rock star numbers as 3.14... and 6.02×10^{23}).

The word dozen comes from the French douzaine (literally a group of twelve) which is a derivation of the Latin word for 12 (douze) with a collective suffix tacked on the end. Now it's perfectly possible to add the same suffix to other numbers and get, say, quinzaine (a group of 15) or centaine (a group of 100), but at least in English, we typically don't.

Because 12 is particularly special.

Mathematically speaking, there's a pretty good argument (if one feels compelled to argue about such things) that counting in a base 12 system (meaning the "tens" place in our numbering system would actually be a "twelves" place) might not be such a terrible idea. We already do it when we tell time, measure in inches, or order a gross of cocktail umbrellas. In the field of finance where calendar months often become an important part of calculations, base 12 (also called "duodecimal" or "dozenal" system by those who actually do feel compelled to argue about such things) could make sense. If we think in terms of factors (the kinds of things mathematicians really geek out about), 12 is a lot more versatile than 10. Ten just factors to 2×5, whereas 12 factors to 6×2, 4×3, and $2 \times 2 \times 3$.

So, I guess it's time to call the babysitter and make a reservation because 12 years gives us a lot to celebrate:

6 jobs x 2 kids = 4 cities x 3 states = 2 advanced degrees x 2 trips to the ER x 3 houses= 12 years of wedded bliss

And I'm looking forward to the next dozen celebrations to come and the next dozen after that. Maybe even a dozen times a dozen; but now I'm getting sappy and (I do apologize for this, but I can't stop myself from typing it) that's just gross.

August 15, 2012

Swimming in Human Infested Waters

You may have noticed that it's Shark Week on the Discovery Channel, that week when we celebrate the most ferocious beast on planet Earth. For 25 years now, the Discovery Channel has been bringing us a combination of fun, educational, and terrifying documentaries about sharks. And it's a great public service they perform, too, since 1 out of every 500 million people die every year from shark attacks.

To put that in some perspective, that means that if the US follows the world trend, that's about 1 lost American citizen every other year! Of course, the US doesn't usually follow world trends. In 2011, a third of the world's shark attacks occurred in the US. Most American shark attacks occur in Florida, a state that (appropriately) serves as home to the International Shark Attack File (ISAF), an organization responsible for authenticating and documenting suspected shark attacks. It makes sense then that the state of Florida has shark attack emergency response down to a science. In 2011, eleven authenticated shark attacks occurred off the Florida coast resulting in zero lost lives.

So I guess what I'm saying is that you probably won't be killed by a shark, and more importantly, if you are, then my odds go way down. In fact, according to Mythbuster Jamie Hyneman, "You're more likely to be killed by: a hot dog, a regular dog, a pig, a horse, a toilet, a vending machine, a black Friday stampede, a lightning strike, a bed, an ant, a game of football, or a roller coaster."

But even under the shadow of this overwhelmingly nonthreatening bunch of (possibly made up) statistics, we somehow remain obsessed with these creatures.

Why is that? The answer, I believe, is fame.

Think about it. The odds of an individual getting gnawed on by a shark (let alone dying from it) might as well be about a gazillion to one, which means if you're one of the few, thanks to the Discovery Channel, you are instantly famous, meaning you might have an entire 15-minute segment of one documentary devoted to your story.

But the shark attack rocket to fame predates Shark Week. The first well-documented case of a shark attack comes from 1749, when 14-year-old Brook Watson, sailor on one of his uncle's merchant ships (and later a member of British Parliament and Lord Mayor of London), was attacked while swimming in the Harbor of Havana. The shark came at him twice, the first time biting off a chunk of his right calf and the second, taking off the foot on the same leg. Crewmembers managed to pull Watson to safety, though he would require amputation of the leg below the knee.

It seems Watson knew what he was doing, though, and he managed to turn misfortune into notoriety. Even though he was born into a good family, Watson was orphaned early in life, leaving his future success uncertain. He proved to be a good merchant and eventually a successful (if not especially well-loved) politician, but that is not why he is remembered today.

Those who recall the name of Brook Watson, most likely remember him for the John Singleton Copley painting which Watson himself commissioned, entitled "Watson and the Shark." The work was a hit when exhibited at the Royal

Academy in 1778. Later, Watson made a great show of bequeathing the work to The Royal Hospital of Christ in London, where it was displayed from shortly after his death until 1963 when it was sold to the National Gallery of Art, where I'm sure you will rush to see it as soon as Shark Week is over.

In his will, Watson went to great lengths to explain that he hoped the painting would serve as a "useful lesson to youth." And it seems to me that's what Shark Week is about, too. I mean, sure Shark Week (and its massive ratings) took the Discovery Channel from a small struggling little cable channel to a huge network that now reaches more than 100 million US homes (at least one potential future shark attack victim) and more than 180 countries, but it's not about the ratings. Like Watson before them, the Discovery Channel is simply attempting to provide a useful lesson to the youth.

So here's what I've learned:

1. There's safety in numbers.

2. Don't bleed.

3. Don't wear or use safety equipment that is "yum yum yellow" (though if we can believe the painting, Watson didn't actually wear anything at all, and that didn't work out so well either).

4. Don't swim in "shark-infested" waters (And definitely don't call it "shark-infested" water. I mean they live there. It's kind of rude.)

5. If you feel you must be attacked by a shark, do it off the coast of Florida.

September 7, 2012

Diet X

My husband and I have recently embarked on a new journey toward healthfulness with the help of P90X. For those of you who are unfamiliar, this program is designed to increase muscle tone and/or mass by working muscle groups in a coordinated way to maximize muscle confusion and give you that beach ready body.

Oh, and it hurts. A lot.

This program is not for the faint of heart, but we knew that going in. Each morning, for almost a week now, we rise long before the sun (a challenge in itself for a couple of night owls) and pop in the day's DVD so that we can huff, puff, and sweat for 60 to 90 minutes before the kids get up and the chaos of the day begins. And that part hasn't been too bad so far.

What I am really struggling with is the accompanying diet. Because with "extreme fitness" comes extreme caloric need. It's not that I can't eat plenty of calories (I think I have mentioned in the past how fond I am of cake), but this is a diet specifically designed to help you build lean muscle. So at the same time that I need to be increasing my calories so I don't "bonk," I also have to strictly limit my carbohydrate intake (so much for the cake) and greatly increase the amount of protein I consume.

Mostly, I eat a lot of meat. I do enjoy meat, and I have

certainly never been a vegetarian; but when I go to Subway, I am just as likely to order a Veggie Delight as I am a Meatball Sub. And I have been known, on occasion, to skip a steak dinner in favor of a salad and an apple. So even though I fully embrace my role on planet Earth as a devoted omnivore, this has been a big adjustment. In fact, between you and me, I think I have a case of the meat sweats.

Though this diet feels a little overwhelming to me, it is actually pretty healthy. Unlike some far more intense carbohydrate elimination diets, P90X does not propose the elimination of any food groups (minus cake); and over the course of the program, the diet shifts back to a much more balanced approach, similar to what I was eating before (still minus cake).

But my struggle with this first phase got me thinking and looking back over history's favorite diet fads, the most revolting of which, for me, is the vinegar diet as popularized by Romantic poet Lord Byron in the early 19th century. (And yes, the tapeworm diet is up there, too, but it's on the list of subjects I'd rather let someone else write about).

The first thing that is important (or at least interesting) to understand about Byron is that he was something of a rock star in his day. Though the works of many of his contemporaries are now usually considered greater than his offerings, Byron was, unlike most of them, truly a celebrity. In fact, shortly after publishing his first work, Byron remarked that he "awoke one morning and found [himself] famous."

In this day and age of overnight stars (thanks to things like reality television and viral YouTube videos), this may sound like a familiar story. Perhaps Lord Byron belonged to the wrong era because the rest of his journey through fame sounds shockingly familiar, too. Byron's legendary promiscuity rivals that of any Hollywood star, and his high profile life included a brief, ill-fated marriage, a love child, an affair with a notable married woman, idealistic political activism, wild mood swings, and a tragically young death.

Overcoming a deformity in his foot, he strived from an early age to excel at sport; and if one can trust the judgment of his contemporary, poet Samuel Taylor Coleridge, Byron was rather easy on the eyes.

But Lord Byron also had a tendency to gain weight (maybe also a fan of cake), which infuriated him, causing him (like many celebrities of today) to take extreme measures to combat any gains. Both anorexic and bulimic, he survived on little more than biscuits and soda water, though he was known to indulge in a raw egg in his tea. Also among his favorites were potatoes, always drenched in vinegar, of which he consumed copious amounts. His celebrity being what it was, the diet spread through the English high society, which (for some reason) prized frailty.

The vinegar diet made a brief comeback in the 1950s when a Vermont doctor by the name of D.C. Jarvis reported that daily doses of apple cider vinegar caused the body to burn more fat. But don't get too excited because although there has never been a study on the effect of vinegar on the human body's ability to burn fat, nutritionists for the most part say there's probably nothing to it. Daily vinegar isn't going to hurt you, but you're going to have to pair it with healthy eating habits and exercise if you expect anything good to come of it.

So as I contemplate the dietary advantages of large quantities of vinegar, I guess I have to come to the conclusion that there are worse ideas than eating a lot of meat. I will stick to my high proteins and low carbs for the next few weeks. If I do, I think I will have to reward myself with a (small) piece of cake. I suppose I can sprinkle it with bacon if I must.

At the Age of 35

In a few days, I will celebrate my 35th birthday. I'm kind of excited about this one because it seems like 35 is the defining age at which a person officially transitions from young adult to adult; and along with that, there is the assumption of wisdom. Now I hope I'm a relatively wise person anyway, but there is something to it. By 35, our bodies are slowing down a little, aching a little more. We start to use phrases like, "Well the sensible thing to do is…." We are finally capable of really imagining our futures and starting to think not just about retirement planning, but maybe even a little beyond. The intemperance of youth has more or less slipped away, and the mature adult has emerged.

In those terms, 35 really might be a sort of milestone. So my birthday has gotten me considering just how I will spend this upcoming year. And to help myself think through that, I'm looking back at the lives of a few notable people and what they were up to at the age of 35.

Though many of the details of William Shakespeare's life and original drafting and publication dates aren't entirely clear, leaving a little wiggle room for interpretation, one could reasonably believe (and for the purposes of this blog post, I do) that in the year 1599, **at the age of 35**, the poet/playwright wrote *As You Like It, Julius Caesar, Henry V*, and possibly even did some early work on Hamlet. He might have written a sonnet or two as well; but as a writer who is not nearly so prolific, I really can't face that possibility.

1811 marked the beginning of Jane Austen's professional writing career with the publication of her first full novel, *Sense and Sensibility*. Although Austen is arguably the most well-known and beloved of women writers in British literature, she gained little attention during her short lifetime. **At the age of 35**, Austen published *Sense and Sensibility* as a novel "by a lady." Not sure I am well-mannered enough to pull off a pseudonym like that.

Known today as the "father of modern genetics," Austrian monk Gregor Mendel gave up on his longtime dream of becoming a high school teacher (after failing the teaching exam several times) and in 1858, **at the age of 35**, turned his attentions instead to pea plants in the monastery garden he tended. His research, which revealed in a very simple way, the pattern by which single-allele traits are inherited from one generation to the next (in retrospect, this guy probably would have made a brilliant high school teacher) was ignored by the scientific community because of Mendel's obscurity. It wasn't until around forty years after his death that his research was rediscovered and promoted, making the name of Gregor Mendel more recognizable the world over than are those of most of his contemporaries who undervalued his contribution to science.

In September of 1882, the Edison Illuminating Company, located on Pearl Street in New York City, fired up a generator that provided electricity to 59 customers. With this event, Thomas Edison, **at the age of 35**, orchestrated the first public use of electricity in the United States. Somehow I doubt, however, that this is the first time a New Yorker appeared lit in public.

Forever an American icon known for his sacrificial leadership in the Civil Rights Movement, Martin Luther King, Jr. was awarded the Nobel Peace Prize in 1964, particularly for his use of nonviolent methods in furthering his cause, even when he himself was threatened by violence. At **the age of 35**, King was the youngest person to have yet been awarded the prize.

On May 25, 1977 (and if you already know why that date is significant, you might be a nerd), George Lucas's *Star Wars: A New Hope* opened in theaters to surprisingly overwhelming success. By Harrison Ford's birthday, almost two months later, **at the age of 35**, he found himself launched from obscure face in a handful of mildly successful films to overnight Hollywood star.

And finally, in more recent news, Misty May-Treanor, **at the age of 35**, won her third Olympic gold medal in beach volleyball at the London 2012 Olympic Games. She and partner Kerri Wash Jennings earned the medal just days after May-Treanor's 35th birthday.

So what will I do **at the age of 35**? I'm afraid I'm not much of a poet; and though I did plant two varieties of pea plants in my garden this year (alas, I forgot to take notes), most likely I will not make any major contributions to scientific understanding. At this point my world is probably a little too small to attract the attention of the Nobel Prize committee. At my best, I am a pathetic actor; and so if I do appear in a science fiction film this year, I'm sure it won't be the unexpected blockbuster with impressively advanced special effects. Sadly, I'll have to wait until I am 38 to have a chance at beach volleyball Olympic glory, and so I'll probably just let Kerri Walsh Jennings and her new partner have that one. If I have my first novel published this year, well, you can be sure I will not publish it quietly under a pseudonym. Forget 35-year-old maturity. I want my credit.

So I guess that just leaves lighting up the night in New York City. I'm going to leave that one on the table as a maybe.

A Classic Blog Post of True Love and High Adventure

In 1569, an Italian master swordsman by the name of Rocco Bonetti arrived in England and promptly set up a fencing college. Much to the annoyance of the London fencing masters, Bonetti charged exorbitant fees for his instruction, which attracted a noble clientele and launched him to great success. The London Masters made no secret of their disdain for Bonetti, whose famous defense was unfavorably referred to in *Paradoxes of Defense* by George Silver, a British master who was a contemporary of Bonetti's.

This professional disregard by his peers seemed not to bother Bonetti much. Clearly not shy about his prowess with the sword, he was a noted trash talker, having once gone so far as to claim that he could cut any button off the shirt of any Englishman with one flick of his rapier. This boast would later be immortalized by William Shakespeare in *Romeo and Juliet*. In Scene 4 of Act 2, Mercutio refers mockingly to Tybalt as "the very butcher of a silk button," which many critics suggest is a clear reference to Rocco Bonetti.

But that is not Bonetti's greatest claim to literary fame. He also appears in *The Princess Bride*, that "classic tale of true love and high adventure" by Florinese literary genius "S. Morgenstern." Most of you will, of course, recognize this work from the "abridgement" by William Goldman that became the greatest movie ever made.

The film celebrated the 25th anniversary of its release at the New York Film Festival this past week. If you don't agree with me that it's the best movie ever made, perhaps you haven't seen it (if you live under a rock or are under the age of 6). Or maybe you just haven't seen it in a long while. If that's the case, you should revisit it. Trust me. You'll love it. Or you'll remember how much you loved it the first 117 times you saw it (I'm giving you the benefit of the doubt here).

On Tuesday, October 2, director Rob Reiner and screenwriter William Goldman gathered with cast members Cary Elwes, Robin Wright, Billy Crystal, Mandy Patinkin, Chris Sarandon, Carol Kane, and Wallace Shawn at a special showing of the film, followed by questions and answers. And even though I couldn't be there in person, in my heart, I was there. Because I have seen *The Princess Bride* way more than 117 times. I literally have every line of every scene from beginning to end memorized and can deliver any of them at a moment's notice. Seriously, you can test me, though I should warn you that my Spanish accent is even more ridiculous than Mandy Patinkin's.

Of all the amazing dialogue in all the great scenes that make me laugh out loud even after 25 years, I think my favorite lines (and I know I'm not alone here) come from the fencing duel between the mysterious man in black and Inigo Montoya atop the Cliffs of Insanity. I love this scene not just for its impressive choreography, but also for the brilliant juxtaposition of a battle to the death with a respectful and practical conversation between fencing masters.

Just in case your memory is a little fuzzy (and for some reason you didn't stop reading in order to immediately go watch it again as soon as I told you to, which is what you should have done), the battle begins after a nice chat in which Inigo allows the man he will soon try to kill a chance to catch his breath. As the two begin to duel (left-handed for an added challenge), Inigo says, "You are using Bonetti's defense against me, uh?" to which the Man in Black replies, "I thought it fitting, considering the rocky terrain." As the duel continues, other fencing masters are casually mentioned as well, including: Ridolfo Capo Ferro, Gérard Thibault, and Camillo Agrippa, all notable masters of their times.

It certainly comes as no surprise to me that *The Princess Bride*, much like this blog, is a well-researched and totally reliable source of historical information. In the past 25 years, numerous fencers and fencing experts have claimed that they started in the sport precisely because they were inspired by the movie. I don't know much about fencing, but *The Princess Bride* has taught me the elements of a great story: fencing, fighting, torture, revenge, true love, and perhaps even a limited amount of kissing. Throw in some wildly imaginative characters and witty dialogue, and you have an instant classic on your hands.

But at this point I'm guessing you still have a couple of questions for me. First, did I really place *The Princess Bride* in the same classic literary category as Shakespeare's *Romeo and Juliet*? Yes. I make no apologies for that.

And second, what became of the talented and arrogant Rocco Bonetti? In 1587, Bonetti engaged in a duel, just outside of his own fencing college, with a man by the name of Austen Bagger. Bonetti died shortly after from wounds received in the duel. Rumors indicate that Bagger was even quite drunk at the time of the battle, suggesting that Bonetti's defense may not have been all it was cracked up to be. Then again, maybe it just wasn't fitting for that particular terrain.

October 18, 2012

High in the Sky Awareness Month

By my count there are 107 different "awareness" titles for the month of October this year, yet I was stunned to find that High in the Sky Awareness didn't make the list. I'd like to make a case for why we should cram just one more celebration into an already very full month. But first, even though I'm sure you're already busy celebrating, let me take a minute to remind you of just a few things of which you should be aware.

If you happen to be Italian-American, German-American, or Polish-American, party it up because this is your month. All the avid readers out there will be happy to know that it's Book Month as well as National Reading Group Month. For the increasingly cynical writers among you, you may wish to note that October is Self-Promotion Month and National "Gain the Inside Advantage Month" (By the way, if you enjoy this blog, please tell your friends about it, especially if you have connections in the publishing industry!)

Also on our radars this month should be a number of conditions and diseases, including: breast cancer, SIDS, RSV, AIDS, celiac disease, Down's syndrome, blindness, and dyslexia. We should be aware of health literacy, which is appropriate because we're celebrating medical librarians this month. Oh, and don't forget to take care of your teeth by focusing on orthodontic health and dental hygiene.

What should you eat while you're observing all that is special about October? Well, it's pizza month; and in case you're stumped trying to choose toppings, it's also sausage month. But don't feel left out if you're vegetarian because October is your month, too, and there are lots of vegetarian friendly celebratory options including: rhubarbs, spinach, pears, pineapples, popcorn, apples, caramel, and American cheese. I realize that last one doesn't work for vegans, but Vegan Awareness Day isn't until November 1st, so I'm not going to let that bother me.

There are many, many more designated awarenesses in the month of October, a few of which I most certainly will not be observing. For instance, October is Caffeine Addiction Recovery Month. You can go ahead and break your caffeine addiction if you want to, but I'm keeping mine.

Still, in this air of intense awareness, we are ignoring one of the coolest things October offers up: the sky. Historically, October has seen some of the greatest advances in the human desire to take to the skies and beyond. Consider, if you will, some of these historic October moments.

As the sun faded on the evening of October 22, 1797, the celebrated French aeronaut André-Jacques Garnerin ascended in a hot-air balloon from the Parc Monceau in Paris to a height of 3000 feet. This in itself was nothing particularly special. For several years, even through the turmoil of revolution, the popularity of the hot air balloon had been growing throughout France, and enthusiastic crowds had watched in awe as unmanned hydrogen balloons reached altitudes of at least 10,500 feet. With a skilled aeronaut aboard, balloons were known to sometimes reach around 6500 feet.

What was really special about this October 22 flight was that at 3000 feet, Garnerin cut through the rope that attached his basket to the balloon; and as it continued to float upward, he began to fall, slowed by the first frameless parachute. Garnerin's original parachute resembled an umbrella in design. It also lacked the air vents that would eventually prove so useful in stabilizing the otherwise bumpy ride caused by the build-up of trapped air under the silk. It seems Garnerin was prone to motion sickness and rumor has it that during this maiden jump, he vomited on the amazed (and unfortunate) crowd. Still, Garnerin survived unscathed; and before long, his stomach settled, and the kinks were worked out of his original plan, allowing for major advancements in parachute design. A mere 33 years later, this allowed Claude Ruggieri to successfully and safely rocket a sheep into the sky.

As impressive as Garnerin's achievements were, however, the October sky wasn't nearly finished yet. By 1905, brothers Orville and Wilbur Wright had been working on glider design and experimenting with powered flight for several years already. On October 5, 1905, they had a major breakthrough. Finally with their third powered airplane design, Wilbur was able to fly a total distance of 24 ½ miles, a success that allowed the brothers to pursue a patent and potential marketability.

But what's really amazing is to think how far flight technology had come by October 14, 1947, when then US Air Force test pilot Chuck Yeager became the first man to break the sound barrier, an achievement he celebrated by doing it again 65 years later (just a few days ago).

Ten years after that first sonic boom, human kind made another leap upward into the sky when on October 4, 1957, the Russian satellite Sputnik launched into orbit. The world held its breath and watched as the first artificial satellite streaked its way across the October sky, inspiring awe, fear, and feverish scientific competition.

And now what else could we possibly do in our October air space? Well, the same day Yeager repeated his historic flight earlier this week, a fascinated world watched as Austrian Felix Baumgartner ascended in a balloon to an altitude of 24 miles, and dressed in a pressurized suit (for some reason I keep picturing Ironman), dove to the earth from the edge of space. The descent took over nine minutes, and Baumgartner landed safely on the ground after becoming the first man to break the sound barrier without a vehicle.

So as you observe National Toilet Tank Repair Month, National Stamp Collecting Month, Squirrel Awareness Month (you apparently only have to be aware of them because Squirrel Appreciation Day doesn't come around until January), and National Sarcastic Awareness Month, take some time to look up at the October sky and think about all the flights of fancy that have become realities of flight in this one amazing month.

October 25, 2012

Why Running is Stupid: Proof that Penguins are Faster than Sock Monkeys

In 490 BC, an important battle raged across the fields of Marathon in Greece between the Greeks and their would-be Persian conquerors, headed ultimately for the city of Athens. According to legend, as the Persians mounted the attack, the Greek army dispatched a runner, most often referred to as Pheidippides, to Sparta to get some much needed help. The run was a breezy 140 miles, and the superstar completed it in about 36 hours. When he was told by the Spartans that they would send help, but could not possibly do so until the appropriate phase of the moon, Pheidippides turned around, Forrest Gump style, and ran the 140 miles back to Marathon to take up arms alongside his fellows.

When the Greeks at Marathon improbably won the battle, even without the aid of the Spartan army, the next concern was to deliver the exciting news to Athens to provide a confidence boost to the city along with a warning that the Persians would soon be coming their way. Since Pheidippides had already so successfully run 280 miles and survived a bloody battle, it seems only natural that he would be called upon again to run the message of victory the measly 25 miles to Athens. Shockingly, he collapsed, dead, as soon as he delivered the message.

Pheidippides ran into the assembly, put his hands on his knees, spitting up a little blood as he tried to gather his breath, and exclaimed: "Something in Greek!" Like most of you, I don't speak Greek, but I'm pretty sure he said something like this: "Wheez...cough...cough...Give me a minute... gag...wheez...Wow, that was a stupid long way to run...cough...Maybe someone should invent the telephone...wheez...gasp...or the telegraph...or smoke signals? Maybe we could get some smoke signals? That might work. 'Cuz I gotta tell you, I can't really feel my legs...gasp...wheez...maybe some Gatorade or water or something? ...cough...Is it getting dark in here?...gag...Oh, and we won...gasp...."

Obviously there are a few things we could learn from the tragic tale of poor Pheidippides. First, if you plan to run a marathon, it may not be in your best interest to run a 280 mile training run first, and you should probably consider not heading into it straight from battle, which, likely, is also quite strenuous. Second, the Greek language is surprisingly efficient. And third, running is stupid.

It's this third point I wish to expand upon; but let me first say, if you are a runner and you read past the title and you've held on this long, thank you. I do not think *you* are stupid. I have the utmost respect for you and all those elite athletes out there who work so hard to achieve their goals. Running may be a great source of joy for you, and I applaud your determination. I do, however, stick to my assertion that running is stupid. Because it is.

Now, you may recall that I have two sons, the oldest of

whom is seven. What I'm not sure that I've mentioned is how amazingly bright my seven-year-old is and like a lot of bright seven-year-olds, E is a voracious reader. So, yes, he reads all the great classics of children's literature (he's working his way through Madeleine L'Engle right now); but he's also just as likely to read nonfiction works, particularly those dealing with science and invention. It doesn't end there, though, because he reads everything that he finds that can possibly be read.

Like fliers. He picks up every single one he sees, without fail, and reads it word for word. So if you are running for political office, raising money for cancer research, or selling gym equipment, you should know that your advertisements are mostly falling into the hands of bright seven-year-olds, which I'm guessing are not within your primary demographic.

So a couple of weeks ago, we're walking through the lobby of the local YMCA after swimming lessons, and E, predictably, can't resist a stack of bright orange fliers that are advertising something called the Monster Dash, a costumed 5 K/1K fun run/walk to raise money for our local Food Share program. E looks it over and says, "Hey Mom, I want to do this." I— lugging the bags full of wet towels and swimsuits; pulling on the hand of my uncooperative 5-year-old; trying to get out of the lobby so that we can make the mad run back home to grab dinner, finish homework, take showers, and get to bed at a reasonable hour — say, without thinking it through, "What's that? For Food Share? Sure. That sounds fun." He, of course, takes me at my word.

Trouble is, I don't run. It hurts my joints. I don't enjoy it. And so, I think it's stupid. That said, I am a fairly active person, and I'm in pretty good shape. I even enjoy the occasional challenge of a race-type event; have completed a sprint triathlon (didn't do the full because it required too much running); and if I could find a biathlon that included swimming and cycling, without the running, I'd be all over it.

On top of this, I am currently about half way through the P90X fitness program, so a little 5 K should be easy, or at least doable. Probably.

Last Saturday, we all got up nice and early, pulled on our Halloween costumes, and headed for the race. My sons, a shark and a ninja, both successfully ran the 1 K kids' run. Then it was my turn. Dressed as a sock monkey, I left the boys and my husband (a banana) and headed to the start line to meet up with my running partner for the day, an 8-year-old daughter of some family friends. This little girl is quite a runner, and she wanted to give the 5 K a try; so since I was committed anyway, I agreed to run with her and keep an eye on her.

And that's how I found myself, running way faster than I ever run (because I don't run), just trying to keep the gap small enough to maintain visual contact with an 8-year-old superstar penguin. I could say that I let her outrun me, but I won't lie to you, my faithful reader.

I may have had an embarrassing run, but I did at least win the funniest costume award; so I guess I can be proud of that, although, I think the gingerbread man was robbed. Most importantly, though, I found out I can run, if I have to. Like perhaps if I have an important message to deliver that will impact the survival of my nation or even the future spread of democracy throughout the world, or if my son picks up a flier advertising a fun run for a good cause.

November 8, 2012

The Patron Saint of Household Slovenliness

Formally canonized by the Roman Catholic Church in 2010, Saint André Bessette spent most of his life as Brother André of the Congregation of the Holy Cross, a generous and humble porter at Notre Dame College in Montreal, Quebec, where he was known for miraculous healings and for his instrumental role in the construction of a chapel honoring Saint Joseph. Today, the Oratory of St. Joseph is a Roman Catholic minor basilica and national shrine located on Mount Royal, overlooking the college.

The ever humble Brother André always credited Saint Joseph with the miraculous healings experienced by those the monk himself blessed, and he was determined to honor the saint. When one of his confreres admitted that he consistently found his statue of Saint Joseph turned from where he had placed it to instead facing the direction of Mount Royal, Brother André knew what had to be done.

Convinced that he had found the right location for Saint Joseph's chapel, Brother André formulated a plan. He quietly planted a medal of Saint Joseph on the land; and for six years, he prayed for the opportunity to purchase the property. In 1896, Brother André's prayers were answered, and the Church of the Holy Cross made the purchase allowing for construction to begin in 1904.

I share Brother Andre's tale because it is an early example of a connection between Saint Joseph and land sales. I have found sources claiming that St. Joseph is the patron saint of cabinet makers, carpenters, engineers, families, fathers, happy deaths, workers, doubters, social justice, travelers, Canada, China, Vietnam, Peru, Korea, and the Universal Church. And yes, according to some, real estate.

This is important to me personally because I am currently trying to sell my house. A little over two years ago, my husband and I packed up our two young sons and embarked on an adventure to the Pacific Northwest. With the exception of a few of my husband's early elementary years, we have both always been Midwesterners. And as much as we have both enjoyed Oregon (except for the rain), it's become clear to us that it is time to head back as 2000 miles (with no direct flights) is a long way from home.

The details of jobs and school are pretty much all falling into place, but one thing remains. We have to sell our Oregon home. If you know anything about the real estate market, you know that, even in a thriving market (which this isn't), fall is not really the best time to try to sell. I suspect that's because no one (except us apparently) wants to try to move all of their possessions in the middle of the snow and ice of winter (or in Oregon, rain). But whatever the reason, in the three weeks that our house has been officially on the market, it's been shown exactly two times.

In some ways that's kind of nice. I don't necessarily want a lot of people traipsing through the house, where I still have to live for a few more months. After all it only takes one showing as long as it's the right one; and if the house remains on the market until spring, I have no doubt the right buyer will come along.

The biggest problem is that it's really hard to stay motivated to keep it clean when we don't have many showings. I wouldn't say we are exceptionally dirty people or anything, but the cleanliness is starting to get to us. For example, the other day, I went to wake up my seven-year-old for school and with chattering teeth, he said, "I'm too cold to get up." When I questioned him about why he was so cold, he said he hadn't wanted to sleep under his covers because then he'd have to make his bed. Oh, honey…

And he's not alone in feeling the added pressure for cleanliness because even though no one is coming to see our house, at any moment, someone could. Maybe even the someone who wants to buy it. Why not? It's a beautiful home: four bedrooms, a bonus family room (with built in electric guitar cabinet!), nicely landscaped yard, in a great neighborhood with really good schools and easy access to the interstate. Someone should want to buy that, right? Seriously, let me know if you are interested.

So I find myself, as I am scrambling to make sure the toothpaste is cleaned out of the sink before I rush the boys off to school every morning, wondering if St. Joseph might put in a good word for us and just get the deal done, so we could stop all this nonsense. So here's how you make the request:

1. Get a plastic statue of Saint Joseph.

2. Bury it in your yard.

3. Make a deal.

Some sources suggest that it might be a good idea to also say a prayer. And various sources suggest different ways of burying your Joseph. He might go right side up, in the front yard facing the "For Sale" sign. Or perhaps he should be lying on his back and pointing toward your house. Some other people insist that that he has to be 3 feet from the rear of the house and/or buried exactly 12 inches deep. Be careful not to let him face away from your house because the house across the street will sell, whether or not it is on the market. And if you're really desperate, bury the poor little statue upside down because Joseph will want to be righted as soon as possible so the deal is sure to happen quickly.

So I wondered what the Roman Catholic Church had to say about all of this. It turns out, this smacks of superstition rather than sound theology; and while the church does approve of honoring the saints and even asking for intercession from them, it frowns on threatening saint statues with eternal internment unless they grant you a favor.

And though I myself am not Catholic, I can see their point. So I guess Saint Joseph is safe at our house, for now. But if traffic doesn't pick up soon, I may find myself following the path of Brother André. Of course, I'm fresh out of Saint Joseph medals, so perhaps I'll have to raid the Little People nativity set.

November 29, 2012

23.7% of People Reading This Have No Idea What "Lumbago" Is

Last Saturday, I sneezed and then I couldn't move. That might sound strange to some, but I'm guessing a fair few of you (some sources suggest about 51.2%, though at least 37.6% of statistics are made up on the spot) have had a similar experience once or twice in your lifetime. Here's the likely familiar story:

I was standing at the bathroom sink, calmly brushing my teeth and lightly stretching out the aching muscles in my low back, which have had the tendency to occasionally get a little sore ever since my second pregnancy (substitute "football injury," "years in the circus," or "shark attack" as may be appropriate for you). As always seems to happen at the most inconvenient times, I felt a powerful sneeze coming on. With toothbrush in hand and with my mouth full of foamy toothpaste, there was little I could do to brace myself for it, so I went with it the best I could. And then the little ache in my back that had been my slightly bothersome companion for several days must have exploded or something because the nuisance ache became something altogether different. It became a screaming knot of angry pain.

So there I was, bent over the sink in front of a toothpaste covered mirror, yelling for help because I couldn't so much as spare a supporting hand to cup a little water and rinse my own mouth without the risk of fainting from the effort.

Luckily, I was not home alone at the time, and my husband soon came to my rescue. He gently cupped water to my mouth to rinse the toothpaste (ah, true love!) and supported me in such a way that I could slowly and painfully shuffle through the bathroom doorway and to a place where I could sit. He fetched me ibuprofen and a heating pad, and to his credit, he didn't even laugh at me all that much.

If you've been in a similar situation (and at least 68.4% of you probably have), then you know that the first thing that goes through your mind when something like this happens is: OW! Next is that list of things you absolutely must get done that have now become impossible. And finally you realize that the pain is so bad, you really can't think what to do about it.

If you lived at least a hundred years ago, the answer would be simple. You'd get yourself some gin.

Gin is nothing more than a simple grain alcohol, flavored with juniper berries and whatever other aromatics one might fancy. Credit for its invention is usually given to a Dutch physician and chemist by the name of Franciscus Sylvius who, in the 17th century, was among the first to suggest that chemical reactions might actually have a great deal to do with the way the body functions. Sylvius was hopeful that gin could relieve stomach discomfort. The medicine soon caught on as a treatment for all sorts of pains, including lumbago (the old-timey word for low back pain).

Another "doctor," identified only as Dr. Sheldon in numerous advertisements from 1915 to 1921, capitalized on the alleged curative properties of gin by claiming that his gin pills could cure lumbago, rheumatism, gout, inflammation of the gall bladder, kidney stones, depression, nervous disorders, fatigue, and possibly even diabetes.

That gin could be used to promote health is not entirely without merit. In the late 1800s and early 1900s, British Royal Navy sailors regularly consumed a cocktail made with gin and lime as a good way to ingest the vitamin C necessary to prevent scurvy. British soldiers serving in India found that if they took the same cocktail and added quinine, their anti-malaria regimen became more palatable. And in the 1920s and early 30s, the United States used low quality homemade gin as a cure for Prohibition.

Gin didn't always enjoy such a glamorous reputation, though. As the cheapest way one could attain alcohol in 18th century England, gin became the driving force behind a great deal of social problems throughout the country. This prompted artist William Hogarth to create his famous etchings, *Beer Street* and *Gin Lane*, which, along with the writings of Henry Fielding, demonstrated that fine, upstanding citizens drink a lot of beer.

Their efforts helped pave the way for the Gin Act of 1751 and forever tainted the reputation of gin in England, which may, in fact, be the reason that the otherwise suave James Bond knows so little about gin that he insists on having his martinis shaken, which those who do know a thing or two about gin will consistently tell you is a big mistake. In Bond's defense, though, he is under a lot of pressure between mastering the use of all kinds of newfangled gadgetry, skydiving with the queen, and making sure his tie is straight.

But even if the aromatics in the gin are bruised and Bond's martini is essentially ruined, it doesn't appear that he is among the 87.3% of the population that suffers from lumbago. Maybe gin has curative properties after all.

In recent years, gin has resurfaced as a remedy for arthritis and joint pain. Though at this point completely unsubstantiated by any scientific study, rumor has it that raisins soaked in gin can offer pain sufferers a great deal of relief. The recipe is simple. Apparently all you have to do is soak your raisins in a small amount of gin and then let the gin evaporate completely before storing your homemade miracle cure in a covered dish in your fridge. Then eat nine of these raisins every day, and you'll be pain free.

Of course, since at least one "reliable" Internet source on which you can find this miraculous recipe also mentions that it takes about a week for all of the gin to evaporate and your raisins to be ready, I didn't think this would be a good option for me. As I sat, unmoving, fighting tears and wondering how I could see my way through the pain enough to function at least a little bit, my need seemed too immediate for the gin raisin cure.

Instead, I opted for a more modern approach: a little heat, some stretching, a lot of ibuprofen, and some doctor-prescribed muscle relaxant at bedtime. Now almost one week later, I am happy to report that without even a drop of gin (which, in case you didn't know, should NEVER be combined with muscle relaxant), I am once again functioning more or less normally.

I'm not ready to run a marathon or anything (not that I ever would), but life among the 95.2% of the population that suffers from occasional lumbago is definitely looking up.

December 6, 2012

"You Better Watch Out; I'm Telling You Why..."

About a month ago my oldest son, now almost eight, asked me a question I had been dreading since he was very small. "Mom," he said. "How does Santa get all those presents to everyone in the entire world in a single night?" Then before I could answer, he gave me a sly look and added, "Unless...but no...do you stuff the stockings on Christmas Eve?" Okay, it wasn't really a question. It was a statement of disbelief; but I went through the motions anyway, just as he had.

"Do you want me to answer that question honestly?" I asked. E nodded, his eyes big, and maybe a little sad. In truth, I was somewhat relieved. Though my husband and I both grew up with strong Santa Claus traditions, I have never been especially comfortable with the whole magic sleigh, flying reindeer, and toy-making elves thing. I want my children to be able to trust that I tell them the truth, and I admit I was concerned Santa Claus would one day be seen by them as a betrayal of that trust.

So I took a deep breath and launched into the story of St. Nicholas, a fourth century bishop known for his quiet generosity and secretive gift-giving. I explained that it is from this story the legendary figure of Santa Claus evolved and that though not literally true, the tale is true enough in spirit and is a celebration of generosity and love that echoes the Divine gift of Jesus, which we celebrate at Christmas.

That's the story I told him because, until very recently, that was the extent of what I knew about the historical St. Nicholas. And then my brother-in-law (coincidentally E's godfather—where was he when we had this tricky conversation?) brought to my attention some new and wonderful information about this celebrated saint.

Born in the late part of the third century in the city of Myra in Lycia (today Demre, Turkey), young Nicholas grew up to become Greek Bishop of Myra. It was in this capacity that he attended the First Council of Nicaea in the year 325. Called by Roman Emperor Constantine, the Council of Nicaea was the first ecumenical gathering of the Christian Church, designed to hammer out a consensus of belief.

At issue, in particular, was the divinity of Christ and his relationship to the Father and the Holy Spirit, on which the teaching of the Church varied widely. At one end of the debate was Egyptian theologian Arius who insisted that Jesus the Son was not equal to the Father and the Holy Spirit. St. Nicholas didn't agree.

As Arius stated his case, Jolly Old Nicholas listened, doing his best to be polite. But, as it does for most of us listening to arguments we don't find credible, his patience wore thin. While Arius continued to drone on, St. Nicholas jumped to his feet and shook his fist (causing his enormous belly to shake like a bowl full of jelly, I imagine). Bellowing a decisive, "Ho Ho Ho," the bishop (his cheeks rosy with anger) crossed the floor and slapped Arius across the face.

Under the authority of Constantine, the other bishops stripped Nicholas of his bishop's robes and threw him, bound in chains, in jail. No longer a part of the council discussions, Nicholas busied himself with prayer and the formation of a naughty list of all the bishops who had turned their backs on his mature and well-formulated argument against Arius's speech. Then the story goes that sometime during the long night, Jesus and his mother Mary appeared to the incarcerated former bishop, released him from his chains, and presented him with fresh robes.

When Constantine heard about the miracle, he released Nicholas from jail, reinstated him as bishop, and informed the rest of the council that they were free to slap Arius as much as they liked. The concept of the Trinity became a cornerstone of Christian theology, and Arius received only a lump of coal for Christmas that year, which taught him a valuable lesson: *Do not* cross Santa Claus because he *will* slap you silly!

Despite my concerns, my son took the explanation of Santa Claus pretty well (even without the inclusion of the jolly old elf's violent tendencies). Familiar as E is with the *Star Wars* galaxy, he recognizes that "from a certain point of view" is sometimes the closest thing we get to truth. Someday I may share with him this other chapter in St. Nicholas's story, though, too, because I also want him to know that there is a Truth worth standing up for, even to the point of a well-timed slap in the face.

The Mother of Lighted Christmas Geese

One cold night in December of 1882, a reporter by the name of Croffet took an evening stroll through a posh district of New York City, where homes had been wired for electric lights. If you're going to take an evening stroll through the city, I'm thinking he probably made a good choice. As he looked at the grand houses, the visiting Detroit reporter was treated to an amazing sight. He wrote:

> There, at the rear of the beautiful parlor, was a large Christmas tree, presenting a most picturesque and uncanny aspect. It was brilliantly lighted with many colored globes about as large as an English walnut and was turning some six times a minute on a little pine box.

Croffet stood at the home of Edward H. Johnson, a long-time associate of Thomas Edison and vice-president of the Edison Electric Light Company. The tree Croffet later wrote about in the *Detroit Post and Tribune* was the first Christmas tree to ever be illuminated with electric lights. By displaying it in his home, Johnson secured his position in history as the "Father of Electric Christmas Tree Lights" (talk about a resumé builder!).

Of course, next to this brilliant accomplishment, poor Edison's own contribution to one of the tackiest of all Christmas traditions, the displaying of outdoor Christmas lights (the top tacky spot is claimed by the musical tie that plays a tinny version of "Jingle Bells"), was sadly outshone (insert groan here). Two years before Johnson's famous tree, Edison lined the outside of his Menlo Park laboratory with festive lights for the holidays. Alas, the only title Edison can claim on his resumé is: "Father of Electricity."

So I confess that I have not always been a huge fan of Christmas lights. When I was younger, I would admit that a few strands on the Christmas tree were quite nice, and if one absolutely insisted, perhaps a thin spattering in a front yard tree was fine. Any more than that just always seemed to me a little ostentatious. But then I met and married my own version of Clark W. Griswold, who believes with his whole heart that "25,000 imported Italian twinkle lights" is a pretty good start.

Like all loving couples with healthy marriages, we had to find a way to work out a compromise. The first few years of our marriage, we lived in a rented duplex, and so we didn't have a great deal of freedom to decorate. Light displays in those days were small. When we finally moved into a house of our own, we decided that we would hit the after Christmas sales every year (because we're cheap) and buy one new lighted decoration to include the next year.

That worked great, because after a few years, lights would need to be replaced, and so the display remained small enough to be a little above my comfort level and somewhere below his wildest imagination. Then a couple things happened. First, LED lights hit the market with a vengeance. Less expensive to operate and longer lasting, these lights have allowed us to hold onto decorations for a much longer period of time.

The second thing that happened is that somehow, little by little, my perception began to shift. I'm not sure why, but I began to look forward to planning and designing light displays. Sometimes I would even alter a driving route to include looking at the lights on other houses to get ideas for what we might do. But I knew I was in real trouble when a few years ago, I suggested, in early December, that we buy a pair of lighted geese for the front yard. With a victory smile on his face, my husband agreed, and the geese went home with us that very day.

This year, however, we are preparing for a big move, and our house is on the market. Because we suspect that not everyone appreciates lighted geese as much as we do, we have toned down our display to a more traditional level. The water fowl remain in the attic above the garage, along with the dancing light lollipops, the strings of blinking candy canes, and the twinkling Christmas trees that normally line the driveway. Christmas is just a little darker at our house this year.

But our tree still shines brightly in the window; and even though it isn't wired to revolve as Johnson's was (he had hoped to be remembered as the "Father of Spinning Christmas Trees," but it didn't stick), I imagine an overly sentimental journalist like Croffet might say it twinkles "like the tree laden with lambent splendor that sparkles above the fountains in Aladdin's palace."

I wonder what he'd say about my lighted geese.

December 27, 2012

Advance Token to the Nearest Railroad

A couple of weeks ago, my eight-year-old son looked through our extensive game collection and asked me to play *Monopoly* with him. I hesitated, thinking he might be too young to grasp the subtleties of such a complicated game, but I told him we'd give it a try.

Inwardly, I giggled with glee at the suggestion. You see, in my family, learning to play the game of *Monopoly* is a rite of passage. I should be clear that it is my family of origin of which I speak here, as my husband has refused to play the game with me since we played once while we were dating, and I crushed him. And gloated.

Please don't think me unsportsmanlike. I am, in general, in favor of fair play and gracious competition. But the game of *Monopoly* is the one exception I make. It brings out my mean streak. Hours upon hours of my childhood were spent first watching my older siblings slowly grind one another into the abyss of total financial ruin on an otherwise lovely Saturday afternoon, and later, participating myself in the epic battle for economic dominance. I have seen my brothers fling the game board in frustration, scattering plastic houses, shiny tokens, and funny money across the room. I have watched as my sister seethes with silent rage when her natural luck runs out, and the game shifts in favor of another player. But still, we always came back for more.

Why did we love it? Interestingly, none of the four of us, though each successfully transitioned into productive adulthood, is particularly involved in the business world. We don't own large tracts of property filled with houses and hotels for which we ruthlessly charge our tenants exorbitant rents. We aren't railroad tycoons, nor are any of us owner/operators of utility companies. And I think I speak for all of us when I say, we've never really wanted to be. So why does this silly game speak to us (and to hundreds of millions of people who have played it since it was first introduced)?

Well, it turns out the answer to that may be found in the history of the popular game. The game of *Monopoly*, as sold all over the world by Parker Brothers, was designed by Charles Darrow in the early 1930s. I say "designed" rather than "invented" because at the time Darrow started producing his game, there had been several similar games floating around already for quite a few years.

Most historians seem to think the earliest of these other games was something called *The Landlord's Game* patented by Elizabeth Magie in 1904. Magie's game, like *Monopoly*, contains spaces that represent properties, which may be purchased and improved, and that generate rent for the owner. The object of the game is also more or less the same, to build up as much money as possible.

The Landlord's Game does contain a few differences, though. The most notable are the inclusion of spaces for Frontier Land, to which any player may retreat at any time during the game. These spaces remain rent and tax free for every player until a specified number of improvements have been made to other properties on the board, at which point players must begin to pay rent on the Frontier spaces as well, though, as the rules are careful to point out, wages never ever rise.

69

Another striking difference between Magie's game and *Monopoly* is the inclusion of "Lord Blueblood," an imaginary character who owns a great deal of the properties, collecting taxes and rent from all players and is not nearly as adorable as the top-hat wearing, much loved Mr. Moneybags. If a player is unfortunate enough to find himself trespassing on Lord Blueblood's private estate, he goes directly to jail and must pay a hefty bail so that he may continue his next turn from the "So What" space next to the jail.

The Landlord's Game, as you may have guessed, had a (barely) hidden agenda. Elizabeth Magie subscribed to the economic theory of Henry George who attributed poverty to the concept of land ownership. Magie designed her game, then, to teach children that the concept of economic competition and land ownership in fact crippled an economy, eventually making most players poor.

For some reason, kids (and their parents) liked *Monopoly* better. Even (and maybe especially) in the midst of the Great Depression from which Darrow's game emerged, the largely impoverished population in the US still dreamed of the opportunity for an individual to work hard, make smart business decisions, generate a little luck along the way, and achieve overwhelming financial success.

The game still ends with all but one victor in total financial ruin. But few refuse to play again after a crushing loss. It seems that most of us still like to take our chances with the promise of potential success. I think I might even be able to convince my husband to play again someday. Of course, now E will be playing, too, and I have to say, the kid is a natural. In our first game, he ruthlessly destroyed me, his own mother. And I was proud of him. Maybe he'll grow up to be a railroad tycoon.

Friday, January 4, 2013

A Practical New Year's Resolution for 2013 (Part 1)

Yesterday, I took a sick day. I always try to post on Thursdays (often very late even by West Coast standards, but Thursday nonetheless). I doubt anyone else even noticed, but it kind of drives me crazy.

Alas, it couldn't be helped because I have the worst cold of my adult life (and yes, I am probably being a bit of an overly dramatic baby, but I don't feel well); and though I was not asleep by the time I would normally have been posting (because it's nearly impossible to sleep when it feels as though your pillow is *inside* your head), I was mentally exhausted.

You see, the family and I just returned from a holiday visit to the Midwest, which included a successful house hunting trip. It also included flights on four different airplanes because the airlines have all gotten together and decided that no one would ever wish to fly direct from Portland to St. Louis. That's four planes (two each way), in the company of four different sets of fellow travelers, with four different collections of germs, and four opportunities to breathe in the infectious

71

soup of recycled air in close quarters.

And this brings me to my New Year's resolution. I've decided that in the year 2013, I will learn to teleport. I'm sure I could use to shed a few pounds, be more productive with my time, get more organized, or whatever; but I really think teleportation is where it's at.

I figure the first step is to determine whether anyone has ever managed to teleport something larger than a subatomic particle. The short answer to that (assuming that you don't count wizards or *Starfleet*) is: no. Well, probably anyway. There's a great conspiracy theory out there that recounts the mysterious 1943 US Navy experiment in which the *USS Eldridge* allegedly teleported from the Philadelphia Naval Shipyard to Norfolk, Virginia, over 200 miles away. The ship is said to have remained in full view of the men aboard the civilian vessel the *SS Andrew Furuseth* before disappearing again and returning to Philadelphia. Oh, and it may also have traveled back in time ten seconds.

The teleportation experiment has never been confirmed by the Navy, whose official response was something like: "Hey, so you chowderheads realize that violates the immutable laws of physics, right?" As for the *Andrew Furuseth*, the master of the ship denied that the crew observed the appearance and disappearance of the *Eldridge*. He was contradicted by only one crewmember who was later shown to have not been on the vessel at the time. Of course, ship records indicate that the *Andrew Furuseth* itself was also not present at Norfolk on the prescribed day, so the story really is probably just a bunch of hokey.

Still, teleportation has been on the minds of conspiracy theorists and science fiction writers since at least 1877 when it featured prominently in Edward Page Mitchell's short story "The Man Without a Body." Since then, characters have been transferred, leaped, bamfed, jaunted, beamed up, and apparated from place to place, frequently with dire consequences. The most well-known, of course, is the terrible fate of Andre Delambre, the unfortunate scientist who managed to turn himself into a fly, proving that there may be fates worse than developing a head cold.

Actually, the more I look into this whole teleportation thing, the more I think I may need to reconsider. Maybe bilocation would be a better option. But that's another post...

A Practical New Year's Resolution for 2013 (Part 2)

So in my previous post, I stated that my 2013 New Year's resolution was that I would learn to teleport. I still haven't ruled out the possibility completely, but there are apparently a few ethical issues beyond accidentally turning one's self into a fly that I hadn't considered before.

The problem is that when an exact duplicate of a teleported object is created, then one of two things must happen. Either the original must be destroyed (sadly, this has already been happening to countless innocent photons in physics labs, and unless concerned citizens like you speak out, the atrocities will likely continue) or the original isn't destroyed and instead exists simultaneously with the relocated duplicate. I don't know about you, but I'm not sure either fate is exactly desirable.

But still, as I think back to the miserable day of travel that it takes to get from Portland to St. Louis by air (two flights; plus layover; plus navigating three airports with two bored, cranky, tired, always-hungry kids who have to pee more than should be humanly possible and can't manage to hold onto their own overstuffed, toy-filled carry-ons for longer than ten minutes at a time; an inevitable mix-up at the car rental place; and a long, dark drive to our final destination), I still might be willing to give it a go. Unless there is a better option.

And it turns out that there just might be. The answer may lie in bilocation, or the appearance of a person in two locations at once. The ability has been attributed to several Catholic saints, the most impressive being Padre Pio of Pietrelcina, Italy, whose many unexplained appearances in multiple locations at the same time have been recorded by a large number of witnesses.

One story claims that during World War II, Padre Pio appeared in the air above the city of San Giovanni Rotondo, where he was serving at the time. The city was under imminent threat of bombing by British and American pilots, but the pilots claim to have observed a robed figure before them in the sky, and all attempts to release the bombs failed. Later, one of the men identified the robed figure as Padre Pio.

Padre Pio was said to have performed a similar bilocation into midair as he guided another pilot's injured air craft into a safe landing, though most recorded incidents of his bilocation are somewhat less dramatic. Typically, the priest appeared to provide comfort and blessings at the deathbeds of many faithful Catholics, often at great distances from his known location.

Though the stories of Padre Pio's bilocation are numerous, they are also highly varied and in most cases not exactly verifiable. And it seems there are a few questions still to consider. For example, if I attend two Thanksgiving dinners in two different states at the exact same time, do I need bigger stretchy pants?

Padre Pio (having apparently never taken the turkey dinner test) said that the bilocator "knows what he wants, knows where he goes, but he does not know if it's the body or the mind that goes." He also claimed that bilocation only occurs when "there is an urgency, a grave danger, a soul or body to save."

As much as bilocation appeals to me (it would be handy with a 2000+ mile interstate move looming, and friends and loved ones on both ends), it is possible that my needs are not urgent enough to qualify. I think I still may give it a try (and maybe save a few innocent photons in the process) because even Padre Pio couldn't help but notice the advantage his bilocation gave to him. When a fellow priest shared with him the unimaginable news that an airplane had made a nonstop flight between Rome and New York in only six hours, Padre Pio smiled and answered, "Six hours! Good heavens, but that is a long time! When I go, it takes me only a second."

January 24, 2013

How Dagwood Split the Atom

In 1907, with a generous loan from his very understanding father, young Alfred Carlton Gilbert (deciding not to use his Yale medical degree) started the Mysto Manufacturing Company, dedicated to the production of magic kits. A few years later, Gilbert traveled by train from Connecticut into New York and while taking in the sights through the train window, mused to himself that the steel girders of a distant building project looked a bit like a toy.

Ever the imaginative chap, Gilbert got to work and soon patented his Erector Set, changing the name of Mysto to the A.C. Gilbert Toy Company. The Erector Set became enormously popular and soon new products emerged, all with the goal of education through play. Before it was a widely accepted concept among early educators, A.C. Gilbert subscribed to the idea that play was how children learned best, and his product line demonstrated it. Gilbert produced not only building sets, but also chemistry sets, microscopes, glass-blowing kits, mineralogy sets, model trains, and even an atomic energy lab.

That's right, folks, in 1950 and 1951 (obviously before the days of the Consumer Product Safety Commission), wealthy parents could purchase for their curious young children the Gilbert U-238 Atomic Energy Lab, complete with a Geiger counter, electroscope, spinthariscope (and if you know what that is, perhaps you played with one as a child), Wilson cloud chamber, four Uranium-bearing ore samples, three low-level radiation sources (and an order form for refills: "Gentlemen: I need replacements for the following radioactive sources, (check which): ALPHA____, BETA _____, GAMMA _____ or CLOUD CHAMBER SOURCE____."), ball and stick model supplies, the *Gilbert Atomic Energy Manual,* three C batteries, and a comic book called *Learn How Dagwood Split the Atom.*

The kit sold for $49.50, which Wikipedia suggests is about 460 of today's US dollars. Of course, you couldn't buy the U-238 for that little today. I found one that sold at auction about a month ago for $8,000 (In today's money that would be around $8,000!).

But I did recently see a mostly complete set on display at the A.C. Gilbert Discovery Village in Salem, Oregon, a children's museum named for the toy inventor who was a Salem native. The museum contains a number of imaginative exhibits, including a display dedicated to A.C. Gilbert's life and work, and a playground in which you can find a play structure that claims to be the largest Erector Set in the world.

I've been to the museum a number of times with my two sons since we live nearby, but this particular visit was at the request of my 8-year-old who received a large Erector Set for Christmas this year. He sorted through the little steel girders, screws, and various other doodads (that's a technical term for those of you who are not as mechanically savvy as I am), and rapidly assembled a crane that lifted all manner of household items. As he worked, I reminded him about A.C. Gilbert and the museum.

Though E certainly did not inherit from me his natural curiosity and mastery of all things mechanical, I am delighted to report that he does share at least a little bit of my interest in research. So to the museum we went, where I geeked out about the fabulously dangerous sounding science kit marketed for only one or two years by the A.C. Gilbert Company and where it turned out that E was actually more interested in climbing all over the giant Erector Set.

He was probably examining it to see how it was put together and perhaps whether or not he would be able to take it apart. I'm sure he would love an atomic energy lab, too. Unfortunately (or not), I don't think you can still get replacement radioactive material without winding up on a government watch list.

February 28, 2013

The All American Camel

Between my former home nestled in Oregon's Willamette Valley and my new home in eastern Missouri is just over 2000 miles of road. Google Maps estimates the drive time at just about 31 hours if you follow the most logical route through Idaho, Utah, Wyoming, Nebraska, and of course, most of the great state of Missouri.

If you want to get really crazy and add a hundred miles or so to the journey, you can swing a little bit south and hit Colorado and Kansas. Either way, it's a pretty drive that will take you through gorgeous mountain passes and wide fields of grazing antelope.

But we didn't go that way. Instead, we began our journey following I-5 South through much of California and then followed Route 66 (roughly, as "the Mainstreet of America" doesn't technically exist anymore) across Arizona, New Mexico, a smidgeon of Texas, Oklahoma, and finally Missouri. For some reason, Google Maps does not recommend this particular route, but then there are a few things Google Maps fails to consider:

1. Northern mountain passes can be quite snowy, and at times, even closed in the middle of February.

2. Repeating routes fails to help my ambitious 8-year-old reach his goal of visiting each of the fifty states in the United States by the time he is an ambitious 25-year-old.

3. As much fun as counting bazillions of antelope can be, the possibility of crossing paths with an Arizona ghost camel is even more exciting.

You may have heard that old rumor that there were once wild camels roaming the Arizona desert. First of all, you can rest assured that this particular rumor is absolutely true, though the camels did not start out either wild or ghostly. Actually, the US Army imported around 75 camels following the Mexican-American War and the accompanying expansion of US territory.

The idea was kind of brilliant. Struggling to supply far-flung outposts in the desert, the army realized that camels might be the perfect solution. They can carry heavy loads, require little water, and will happily graze on much of the rough desert plants that cause horses and mules to turn up their noses. But they do have a few drawbacks as well. Unfortunately, they have a habit of wandering far and wide to graze, tend to spook other pack animals, and have hooves that are much better suited to fine grains of sand than to the rocky terrain of the Painted and Mohave deserts, which often rendered them lame.

In the end, the army abandoned the experiment (to be fair, the Civil War probably gave it bigger things to think about than camels), auctioned what camels it could (alas, for some reason the demand was somewhat lower than anticipated), and simply released the rest.

Enter the era of wild camels roaming the Arizona desert. The camels seemed to do pretty well for themselves, and no one outside of a few overexcited hunters paid them much attention, except in the case of one very large beast dubbed

"Red Ghost." The first encounter with Red Ghost occurred when a woman was found trampled to death. Next to her, witnesses found large camel prints and tufts of reddish fur.

Not long after, a couple of camped out miners reported seeing the beast with what looked like a dead rider on its back. Again, the Red Ghost left behind a few hair samples and his very large footprints. Soon more witnesses were getting in the game, one group insisting that they watched as something fell from the camel's back and upon further inspection, found that it was, in fact, a human skull.

When, in 1893, an Arizona farmer shot the reddish animal as it grazed in the man's garden, the apparently dead and now headless rider was no longer atop the camel's back, but a saddle complete with unusual leather straps remained. No one ever determined the identity of the rider who, I think we can assume, met with a pretty terrible end.

But even though the last wild American camel is thought to have died by 1934, rumor has it that one might occasionally spot the Red Ghost and his headless rider wandering through the deserts of Arizona. Whether the witnesses are all stranded motorists who forgot their bottles of Evian, I can't say. What I do know is that having recently followed the trail myself (thankfully not on the back of a camel), I would have welcomed a change of scenery. Sadly, we didn't spot the ghostly pair on our drive, but my son did manage to mark off four new states, and we did see a field full of antelope.

Rollin' With My Homies

With our recent move has come the transition for my children into a new school system. Fortunately, we have found ourselves in what appears to be a very active school and district. This is nice because even though a large part of our family is within a relatively easy drive, we don't really know anyone in our new town yet. So, logically, we have tried to take advantage of all the program opportunities to get out there, meet some folks, and ensure that our boys don't fall into an antisocial stupor.

It's good for them to get out there. But what it means for me, is that just the other night, I experienced my first elementary school Skate Night. Actually I should clarify that it was my first as a parent. I well remember the skate nights of my own elementary days. My hometown had a very nice (I didn't appreciate how nice at the time) roller skating rink, and each of the grade schools in the area participated in a monthly skate night to raise money for the school.

For those of you whose schools had similar events, I'm sure I don't have to tell you that it was THE event around which the entire elementary social structure was based. As the night approached, a flurry of notes (mostly the kind that ask you to check a box) made the rounds through classrooms, deals were made and broken in the dark corners of the lunch room, and desperate girls and boys volleyed for social position around the single most important question: Who would couple up for the moonlight skate at the end of the night?

It was a magical event. A time when a geeky nobody could show up in all the right clothes (tight-rolled Guess jeans and a Hypercolor shirt), just the right moves (you can skate backwards…on purpose?!), and a pocket full of cash to blow on the juke box and a plate of nachos to share with that someone special who against all odds might venture out onto the floor with you. The mighty could tumble (literally), and heroes could rise on Skate Night.

Fortunately, my boys are still in kindergarten and second grade, so they aren't into all the drama just yet; but I know it looms on their horizons. As I walked into the roller rink, I expected to be flooded with memories (both good and bad) of Skate Nights from my past, but it didn't happen. I mean, the drama was certainly playing out just as I remembered it, and I can't deny that I smiled as I watched the groups of fifth-grade boys and fifth-grade girls shuffle around one another in a dance that I'm pretty sure my generation choreographed.

But three much bigger memories flashed through my mind as I helped my boys lace up their skates:

1. A neighbor from a few years back took his children for their first time roller skating. He returned home two days later after surgery to repair his torn patellar tendon. A few months later he could walk again.

2. A few months ago a friend from my college days took her children for their first time roller skating. After surgery on her broken ankle and a lot of painful therapy, she is more or less walking again.

3. My own mother, having made it through first Skate Nights with three children already, accompanied

her youngest daughter onto the floor and was immediately involved in a collision that resulted in a badly sprained wrist. She enrolled me in lessons and never skated again.

Although it always seems like a pretty good idea at the time, perhaps it shouldn't come as a big surprise that strapping wheels to our feet has not always worked out so well for humankind. And I'm guessing that the first person to ever have his name associated with the roller skate probably wished he'd never tried it.

John Joseph Merlin (born in Belgium in 1735) was a very talented inventor. He first made a name for himself as a maker of clocks and other mathematical instruments in France. Later, he would continue his successful career in London, where he would build wheel chairs, invent a barrel organ, improve upon many existing stringed instruments, and design simple robots that inspired Charles Babbage (whose invention became the forerunner of the modern computer) when Babbage was just a young boy.

But for all of his successes, John Joseph Merlin's name is most often remembered as the man who in 1760 literally crashed his way into the London social scene on a pair of roller skates of his own invention.

An accomplished violinist, Merlin had been invited to play at a masquerade ball in London. In order to make a memorable entrance (I mean, lots of people can probably play the violin, right?), Merlin strapped a line of metal wheels onto his boots and rolled his way into the ballroom, straight at the very large, very expensive mirror that adorned one wall, and remembered that he had forgotten to install brakes.

The mirror crashed around him causing serious injury to Merlin, his violin, and to the roller skating industry, which, after that stunt, didn't gain much traction (if that's even possible) until the early 1900s and didn't ascend to the very height of fashion until the Disco Era.

I am happy to report that I fared better than did my neighbor, my friend, my mother, and John Joseph Merlin. I didn't break any bones and neither did the boys. Though I am also thankful that the little one thought strapping wheels to one's feet turned out to be a pretty stupid idea, and he's not anxious to do it again.

If my older son felt the same way, he didn't say so. He came home tired and maybe a little battered and bruised, but there was a strange gleam in his eye, like maybe he had just begun to glimpse the social possibilities of Skate Night; and I'm betting he's not going to want to miss out. Maybe I should get him enrolled in some lessons.

March 14, 2013

Yielding the Circumference

Today is March 14 (3/14 in the US), which means that millions of nerds are spending the day happily celebrating that most mysterious of irrational numbers, *pi*. I'll just briefly explain in case you don't happen to be a nerd (because the jury's still out). *Pi* (which is a stage name because this rockstar number is too irrational to have it any other way) is the expression of the ratio of the circumference (the distance around) of a circle to the diameter (the distance across and through the center) of that same circle.

Ancient nerds discovered that this ratio is constant for any circle, and like nerds will do (and this is the reason they generally make more money than non-nerds), they correctly decided that this might be information worth noting. And when I say "ancient," I'm talking *before* Egyptians and Babylonians started writing down their various approximations for this handy little ratio, say 4000 years ago.

In fact, I think it's safe to suggest that the approximate value of *pi* was probably discovered first by the same caveman (let's just call him Og) who invented the wheel. He carefully painted the number (out to 300 decimal places) on a yet-to-be discovered cave wall and proudly showed it to the other cavemen because he thought it was so neat. At that point (and again, I'm just assuming here), the other cavemen gave Og a wedgie.

Don't fret, though. Og didn't suffer in vain because humankind has been using his handy little observation ever since and has spent thousands of years approximating the constant. After the Egyptians and the Babylonians, who each found the number to be a little more than 3, *pi* shows up in the history of India and China (where again it was found to be a little over 3).

It also gets a nod in the Hebrew Bible (in 1 Kings 7:23) where it is calculated to be 3. This has (believe it or not) been a source of great controversy for Hebrew scholars, but what I think it indicates is that God isn't all that impressed by our efforts to calculate *pi* out to well over 10 trillion places. This may also be illustrated by the fact that if one were to calculate the circumference of a circle that enclosed the entire known universe (you know, just for fun), using just 39 decimal places of *pi* would yield an answer with a maximum error equal to the radius of a hydrogen atom.

Still, I suppose it's nice that thanks to computers, we can now calculate the value of *pi* is a little bit over 3. Most of us (at least those of us who aren't mathematicians by trade) never bother with much more than 3.14. So on March 14 we release our inner nerd (some more inner than others) to celebrate by baking and eating pie because if we can't be bothered with all those extra decimal places, we sure aren't going to be concerned by an extra (delicious) "e" at the end.

One question that remains for me, though (because my inner nerd is actually more interested in symbol origins than in geometry), is why is this super important irrational constant referred to by the Greek letter π? The answer is pretty simple. Before it had a stage name to call its own, *pi* was referred to most often as *"quantitas in quam cum multiflicetur diameter, proveniet circumferencia"* or "the quantity which, when the diameter is multiplied by it, yields the circumference." Admittedly this name is highly descriptive, but probably a little cumbersome written into an equation.

In 1706, a Welsh math teacher by the name of William Jones first introduced π as the now universally recognized symbol for this precise meaning. Though Jones isn't well remembered for any other contributions to mathematics, Leonhard Euler (who was a heavy hitter in the field) adopted and popularized the symbol. It was chosen simply because in Greek, π is the first letter of the word for perimeter.

And I suspect that it was chosen because no one could figure out what to eat in order to celebrate Yielding the Circumference Day. Whatever you call it, it's a day for all of us nerds (and, yes, if you stuck with this post until the very end, the jury is done deliberating) to enjoy a piece of *pi*E. I'm thinking cherry.

A Case of Mistaken Identity

On September 27, 1947, a telegram arrived at the home of Finnish American Architect Eliel Saarinen announcing that he had been chosen as one of five finalists in the design competition for the Jefferson National Expansion Memorial in St. Louis. A successful and well-respected architect already, Eliel probably seemed like a logical choice, and this was no doubt a sweet moment for him. Upon receiving the telegram, the family broke out a bottle of champagne to celebrate.

Spirits were indeed high in the Saarinen household. Then about two hours later, a competition official called to explain that a mistake had been made. Eliel's design had not been selected among the five finalists. That honor had gone, instead, to his 37-year-old son, budding architect Eero Saarinen.

Upon receiving the news, Eliel swallowed any disappointment he might have felt and broke out another bottle of champagne to toast to his son's success. A few months later, the selection committee chose for the memorial Eero's design, his first major project without his father's assistance.

And I have to assume that Eliel was (despite any

90

expletives that undoubtedly leapt to his mind at some point) incredibly proud of his son who was following so successfully in his footsteps. Eero Saarinen would go on to design such major projects as Washington Dulles International Airport, the US Embassy buildings in London and Oslo, the TWA flight center at JFK Airport, and many, many others. But it all started with that simple arch that gives the relatively small city of St. Louis, Missouri one of the most recognizable skylines in the world.

With his design, Eero Saarinen set out not only to commemorate Thomas Jefferson, the Louisiana Purchase, and the beginning of national westward expansion, but also to mark his own time with a wholly unique structural form. In his own words, "at the edge of the Mississippi River, a great arch...seemed right."

He's not entirely wrong. Growing up within a couple hour radius of St. Louis and now returning to the area as an adult, I agree that something about the Arch just seems right. One can look up at it and almost imagine Lewis and Clark pulling out a pair of comically oversized scissors and snipping an expansive red ribbon before marching through the world's largest croquet wicket to begin their westward journey.

But Eero Saarinen misspoke, too, because the Gateway to the West is not, in fact, an arch at all. As many know-it-alls can tell you, the Arch is actually a modified inverted catenary curve. In case you don't remember everything you learned in high school trig class (though I'm sure you do), a catenary curve is the shape made when a chain is suspended from two points and allowed to hang freely. It looks a little like a parabola (but it's not); and if you turn it upside down and modify it to have thicker bases and a narrower top, then you have the shape of the St. Louis "Arch."

Of course this only matters to a handful of know-it-alls. One of those happens to be my dad who worked for many years as everyone's favorite high school geometry and trigonometry teacher. Go ahead and ask me the definition of a function (just be warned that I'll have to sing it to you to the tune of "The Battle Hymn of the Republic").

As it turns out, it also mattered to the first boy I ever brought home from college to meet my parents. Somehow the subject of the Arch came up in conversation, and my relatively new know-it-all boyfriend said, "Well, of course, really it should be called the Gateway Inverted Catenary Curve." It seems the boyfriend knew his audience. I'm pretty sure he would have eventually impressed my dad anyway (this know-it-all boyfriend is now my know-it-all husband, and the two of them get along splendidly), but there's little doubt in my mind that it was love at first catenary curve.

This was also true for the committee charged with choosing the design for the Jefferson Memorial. The vote was unanimous in favor of Eero Saarinen's design because it just seemed right; and for most of us, whether you call it an inverted catenary curve or an arch doesn't really matter. Just make sure you call the right architect.

How I Became a (Mostly) Crazy Fish Lady

About five years ago, my husband suggested we join the estimated 10 million other American households that maintain at least one aquarium full of fish. I agreed mostly because it seemed easier than getting a dog, but also because I had one of those small three gallon hexagonal tanks in my bedroom as a kid, and it was kind of cool. Also, we had recently visited a friend who had a hundred and something gallon tank built into a dividing wall in his basement, and I have to say, it was exceptionally cool. So I thought a 10-20 gallon aquarium could be a nice addition to our home.

What I failed to anticipate was that my husband would call our fish-obsessed friend for advice. What he was told was "go big or don't bother." Oh, I suspect he also got a few pointers on how to convince your wife you need a bigger aquarium than you originally discussed. I don't even know how he pulled it off (except I do distinctly remember that he agreed to clean the thing), but a few hours later, we were driving home with a 65 gallon aquarium strapped into the back of the minivan.

Maybe a week after that, we had a fully functioning home aquarium, about half a dozen small tropical freshwater starter fish (conventional wisdom suggests you need a gallon for each inch of fish so we had some room to grow), and absolutely no idea what we were doing.

Really, though, how hard could it be? People have been keeping live fish for thousands of years, starting with the Sumerians around 2500 BC. These first fish were food rather than pets, maintained in shallow sea-side pools. In Ancient China, captive carp breeding for food was well-established by at least 475 BC. Over the years, this led to the keeping of goldfish in outdoor ponds purely for aesthetic pleasure, a practice that was well established in China by the time of the Song Dynasty (960-1279). From China, the art of keeping and breeding goldfish spread to Japan and eventually to Europe by the late 17th century.

But it's the relationship that the Romans had to their fish that I find most interesting. Wealthy Romans were also in the habit of maintaining fish ponds sometimes as a food source, but more often as a show of wealth. They also tended to have a few favorite fish that they treated more like pets. And we're not talking about fluttery goldfish, bred for optimum beauty. Mostly, the Romans kept things like lampreys and eels, which looked like, well, lampreys and eels.

To compensate for the lack of natural beauty, the owners would decorate their favored fish with jewelry piercings and beaded necklaces (but only if they had offended the fish somehow and needed to apologize). One story even goes that Lucius Licinius Crassus (140-91 BC), a respected orator and Roman censor, went into deep mourning upon the death of his favorite fish. (Again, this is an eel. Wearing earrings.)

Allegedly the distraught fish breeder built a tomb for his beloved pet. When taunted publicly by fellow censor Gnaeus Demetius Ahenobarbus, Licinus defended his behavior by accusing Demetius of being so emotionally barren that he had buried three wives without shedding a single tear. It seems that Demetius also did not challenge the truth of his colleague's statement, which, I suppose, does make him creepier than the overly attached fish whisperer. This round goes to Licinus in my book.

We've had our share of fish death in our tank over the years. Of course, it's going to happen when you're dealing with animals that don't have a particularly long life span anyway and that are really sensitive to their environment, which is controlled entirely by an incompetent person.

I will say this, though, I have come a long way these last five years (thank goodness for the Internet). For someone whose previous aquarium experience included accidentally cooking a black tetra by turning up the heater too high and whose husband has never once cleaned the 65 gallon fish tank, I think I've done pretty well. I have certainly learned a few things:

1. A little algae isn't going to hurt, and it is possible to clean an aquarium too much, unless, for some reason, you want to grow blue/green death bacteria.

2. Big fish will eat little fish, no matter how community-oriented the store's labels may claim them to be.

3. Fish eat about half as much as you think they do, and they poop at least twice as much as you think should be possible.

4. Dirty fish aquarium water is not particularly harmful to toddlers if ingested in the 1.5 seconds while Mom's back is turned.

5. Snails are gross and probably inevitable.

6. Kids don't view fish as actual pets for very long and will eventually beg you for a guinea pig.

I will also grudgingly admit that our new house feels much more like home now that the aquarium has been back up and running for almost a week. After two cross country moves, countless hours of maintenance, A LOT of failure, and some successes, too, I think I have finally come to appreciate our fishy monstrosity. And I hope that our four new, tiny, little tester fish enjoy their new home as much as I do. I have taken a lot of care in preparing it for them and for their fishy friends yet to come.

It's been three days, and I am delighted to report that none of them have died yet. If they do, I'll probably mourn them. But I am not buying them jewelry.

April 25, 2013

History Best Served with a Glass of Milk

This week marked the beginning of the main spring fundraiser at my sons' school. What this means is that my neighborhood has been invaded by an army of adorable door-to-door salesmen. Children packing full-colored brochures full of glossy photos of fresh-baked cookies launch their indefensible attacks every day as they walk home from the bus stop.

And I can't say no, right? I mean they are peddling 2.7-pound tubs of cookie dough in 22 varieties, most sporting names that make my mouth water. Of course, I *need* giant tubs of cookie dough. I can put them in my freezer and pop out just a little bit to make a small cookie snack. And I'll have several varieties to make a mix of delicious cookies for a family gathering or an upcoming road trip. That will totally work. I will *not* sit down in front of the TV with a tub full of cookie dough and a spoon.

I could resist it. I work out regularly and more or less watch what I eat. I take care of myself, but I do occasionally tire of listening to the little health nut that lives inside my head. Sometimes I'm ready to let the cookies step in and take over for a while.

I'm guessing that I'm not alone in this experience, and that perhaps, even you, dear reader, have allowed cookie mania to invade your brain from time to time. Actually, it occurred to me that this phenomenon is not entirely new in the course of human history, either. It might even be the elusive explanation for a piece of history that isn't well understood.

In AD 711, Berber general Tariq ibn Ziyad invaded the Visigoth-controlled Iberian Peninsula. The Visigoths had been in charge for about 300 years at that point, and rumor has it, no one liked them very much. Making up only a small percentage of the population of the region, the Visigoths most likely ruled with brutal force, but ultimately they had little cultural influence on the region because with no written language of their own, there were very few Visigoth bloggers.

Not a whole lot is known about the invasion outside of a few tales that were most likely constructed many years after the event (by Moorish bloggers, which just like their modern counterparts had the tendency to exaggerate or on occasion even make things up), but one thing that does stick out in the history is that the invasion didn't take that long. In fact, it was kind of easy. Some tales even suggest that the Berber army was invited into the region by enemies of the Visigoth's King Roderick.

The invaders killed the king, and with the army in disarray, the Iberian Romans seem to have been uninterested in stepping up to defend themselves from their newest conquerors. So as the defeated Visigoths laced up their corsets, donned their trench coats, stained their lips black, and started hanging out behind the high school gymnasium, enter nearly 800 years of rule by the Islamic Moors in the Iberian Peninsula.

Unlike the previous conquerors, the Muslims had an enormous impact on the culture of the region. Today their influence is seen most dramatically in the architecture, art, and bits of language they left behind in Spain. They developed a highly advanced society, becoming a world center for education and the exchange of ideas, while making great strides in agriculture, science, and, most importantly, cookies.

This is the one main point that I believe historians have tended to overlook. No, we don't have very reliable sources that explain why the Berbers pushed their way into the Iberian Peninsula, and we can really only make some good guesses as to why they so easily conquered the ruling Visigoths. What we do know is that this invasion marks the introduction of the cookie (originally developed in Persia) into Europe.

I don't know about you, but I find it difficult to resist anyone who brings me cookies or even the promise of a tub full of cookie dough in imaginative flavors for which I have no recipe, like Extra Chunky Chocolate with Reese's Pieces. Fifteen dollars you say? You want to defeat the Visigoths and rule the land, you say? I'm sold. Hand me a spoon.

Relentlessly Pursued by Vampires

School is out, and my boys have almost two weeks of sleeping in, fighting, swimming, fighting, fishing, fighting, baseball, and fighting under their belts. I'd say we're off to a pretty good start; but before all of that summer fun could get under way, we had to get through the end of school chaos. And by that, of course, I mean Field Day.

I have to give our school some credit, though. It was almost kind of controlled chaos. No one got hurt, and I think fun was had by all (except maybe the teachers in the dunk tank on a chilly overcast day). I even sort of enjoyed it, too.

I had an especially important job: I ran the marble grab game. Basically, there was a wading pool filled with water and about a ton of marbles. Two kids at a time raced to see who could grab the most marbles with their toes and dump them into a cup at the side of the pool. (Future Olympic sport?) We're teaching important life skills here, people!

So what I had to do was keep the timer, wrestle kids into some semblance of a straight line, occasionally catch a stumbling youngster, and chase stray slimy, toe jam-covered marbles. I know what you're thinking, but believe me when I say, it wasn't nearly as glamorous as it sounds. At least I did have a partner.

My partner was a mother of a kindergartener who was in the same class as my youngest, and it was a pleasure to team up with her for the day. It turned out we had a lot in common:

1. Obviously we are both great moms (because we let ourselves get suckered into helping with Field Day)

2. We both found the increasingly dirty water in the wading pool pretty much revolting.

3. We are both creative problem solvers ("Bonus points if you pick up the slimy marbles in the grass!").

4. We are both being relentlessly pursued by vampires.

As professional as my partner was, she did receive a phone call while on duty. To her credit, she didn't answer (one simply can't run a tight marble grab game if not 100% focused on the task). Instead, she rolled her eyes and commented, "Ugh. It's the Red Cross again. You ever have an organization just hound you until you can't stand it?"

I was, of course, completely focused on the battle before me as two second grade girls with apparently freakishly long toes locked in an epic struggle with only five seconds to go (I was expecting bloodshed), but I admit, her question resonated with me and my focus was temporarily broken. "Oh, yes," I replied. "I get that from the Red Cross in Oregon."

Because about four months ago I relocated from Oregon to St. Louis and I am also a mostly dedicated blood donor. Before having kids, I was committed to donating every eight weeks. Since kids, I am busier, but I still try to give blood about three or four times a year. I am youngish, healthy, don't suffer from an irrational fear of needles, and have never gotten a face tattoo, so I feel like donating blood is an easy way to help out my fellow man.

And the American Red Cross does a bang-up job of collecting, screening, and distributing pints of blood so that those who need it have access to it. After all, they've been doing it since February 4, 1941, when the first American Red Cross blood donation center opened in New York. Over the course of World War II, the Red Cross vampires (or as some might call them "phlebotomists") collected a whopping 13 million units of blood.

The American Red Cross was not the first organization to collect blood in this way. As early as 1922, there was a small-scale blood collection center run from the London home of Percy Lane Oliver, who was not a doctor, but served as honorary secretary of the Camberwell division of the British Red Cross. Oliver saw a need for a unified effort to collect and distribute donated blood to hospitals.

And though the processes for storing and using donated blood were not yet perfected, Oliver's small center conducted health history screens of possible donors (those without face tattoos), conducted rudimentary typing, and established lists with contact information; so donors could be reached whenever there was a need.

His approach caught hold, and as World War II increased the demand for blood, the American Red Cross developed a similar approach. Today, there is a wide system of inter-connected blood collection centers throughout the US; many of which are run by the Red Cross, which collects and tests blood, asking potential donors intrusive, personal questions, such as: "In the last year, have you gotten a tattoo on your face?"

They also keep phone numbers, and when there is a need, they call. A lot. And if you have ever donated, even once, they call. Regardless of whether or not you have a commitment to monitor the marble grab training efforts of future Olympians, the Red Cross vampires will call. If you tell them you have moved out of state, over 2000 miles away, they call again the next day. And if you've recently gotten a tattoo on your face, they'll call again in a year.

I can't blame them, exactly. It's a great thing they are doing; and with only about a third of the eligible American population actually donating each year and an endless need for blood, it's a big job getting those of us who are willing to walk through the door often enough to meet the demand.

I am very grateful for the work they do because it means that if tragedy should strike during Field Day (which would obviously not happen at the marble grab game because that one has some pretty top-notch volunteers), the area hospitals will be prepared. But man are those vampires relentless!

So here's what I say. Unless you use heroin or have received a blood transfusion in a third world prison system, please, please, please donate a pint of blood. Then if you ever intend to volunteer for Field Day, make sure you donate every eight weeks. And whatever you do, never, ever move out of state, unless maybe you plan to get a tattoo on your face.

May 13, 2013

The Accidental Discovery of Family Pizza Night

After spending several weeks sailing around the islands of the West Indies, on October 28, 1492, Christopher Columbus discovered the island of Japan. When I say "West Indies," what I mean is the Bahamas; and by "Japan," I mean Cuba. Actually, you might take issue with the word "discovered," too, since there were already quite a few people living there.

So despite the fact that Columbus was something of a navigational superhero, he had a few things mixed up. Although you've probably heard rumors to the contrary, Columbus was most likely pretty sure the world was spherical because most educated people since Aristotle had at least that much figured out. Where the Italian explorer went wrong, however, was in his drastic underestimation of the earth's circumference. The circumference had, in fact, been fairly accurately calculated as early as the 3rd century BC.

But Columbus wisely rejected these older calculations (which were based on such unreliable techniques as stellar observation and basic trigonometry), and in his own words, "did not make use of intelligence, mathematics, or maps." And it turned out to be a good call because had he not headed west in search of a better trade route to the East, he never would have been the first European to discover America (which he totally was as long as you don't count Leif Ericson); and two of the earth's seven continents wouldn't be named in his honor (which they're not because of his lifelong refusal to admit he had reached an entirely new land mass, even in the face of mounting evidence).

So it's easy to poke a little fun at the just-a-little-off accomplishments of Christopher Columbus; but if I'm really honest with myself, I kind of relate to the guy. You see, I am what you might call (if you're being exceptionally kind) a little directionally challenged. If you're taking a road trip, I am not the one you want holding the map. In fact, you probably shouldn't let me drive much either if there's any chance you might fall asleep because if you do, we'll end up in Oklahoma (assuming that's not where we're planning to go).

As you can no doubt imagine, this can be a little bit of a problem when moving to a new community, which my family and I have recently done. Yes, there is technology out there to help people like me, and I do have a Garmin in my car. It's helpful, sort of. The trouble is that we lived in Oregon's Central Willamette Valley for almost three years; and I found that, surrounded by mountains on two sides and a nearby north/south running interstate, I never really needed it that much. For the first time in my life, I had a little bit of clarity with regard to direction. I kind of felt like a navigational superhero.

Alas, the Midwest is my kryptonite and the Garmin's maps were last updated like three Interstates ago, meaning that most of the time she (because her name is "Ms. Nuvi") doesn't know where I am any better than I do. I keep meaning to get the update; but honestly, my boys and I really enjoy it when Ms. Nuvi recalculates. And when she tells us to take a U-turn because she thinks we've driven into a lake, the giggles that result are well worth some occasional disorientation. For now, I'm on my own.

I haven't done as badly as I feared I would. I have almost

always found a way to get where I am going. That was until this past Monday. My youngest has been taking swimming lessons for quite a while now (and not to brag or anything, but we're coming for you, Michael Phelps). When we moved, I figured out pretty quickly where we could find the nearest YMCA and got him signed up. I found it okay, just a quick hop down an interstate and then a couple of turns on some fairly straightforward highways. That worked great for a couple of weeks.

Then on Monday, we were running late. It happened that my husband had recently attended a meeting near the YMCA and had casually mentioned that he'd taken a different route that he thought saved him a little time. Navigational superhero that I still think I am, I decided to try it.

Fifteen minutes after swimming lessons started (without my future Olympian), I asked Ms. Nuvi to show us the way home, which, thankfully, she was able to do. To my dismay, my husband was home from work already when the boys and I walked in long before we were due to arrive. He took one look at my dejected expression and gave me a hug because he realized that there will be plenty of time to make fun of me later.

But just like Christopher Columbus's so-called discovery of America, there is a bright side to my story. Because I was bold enough to try a new route that didn't pan out quite as I had hoped, we had a little more time that evening than we otherwise would have. What we did with that time (because obviously I was way too upset to cook dinner) was try out a local pizza place that I was clever enough to "discover." A couple of slices of buffalo chicken pizza later, I was pretty sure I had ended up exactly where I'd meant to all along.

May 23, 2013

A Shameful Secret and a Silly Hat

It's graduation season, when scores of students polish up final papers and cram for those last exams all in hopes that the next big thing will be even better than what they have just worked so hard to complete. Graduation is indeed a big deal, deserving of a large celebration with family, friends, cake, and a very silly hat.

Historians can fairly comfortably trace the roots of the traditional square graduation cap (commonly referred to as a mortarboard or a trencher) all the way back to the early 14th century, and no one is ruling out that the history may go back further than that. Likely evolving from the headwear of clergy, peculiar caps started showing up on the heads of the most prestigious of academics in the earliest English-speaking universities. Typically, the more important the academic, the sillier the hat (because nothing says "I'm smarter than you" like absurd headwear).

But because it's hard to see someone in a goofy hat and not want one for yourself, it wasn't long before lesser scholars (like English majors) began to don flat-topped square caps (the particularly rebellious ones bedazzled the tops with brilliantly coded messages such as: *Hi Mom*).

Today the caps, complete with tassels (an accessory added

sometime in the 18th century), are worn by academics throughout much of the world; but outside of Oxford and Cambridge (which appear pompous and circumstantial when compared to their more casual counterparts), the full academic dress is reserved for graduation ceremonies. Every spring, graduates (from PhD recipients to high school seniors) line up in their ridiculous hats.

Apparently even Kindergartners get in on the action, and I have to say, I am a little bitter about it. I'm going to reveal one of my deepest secrets to you, my faithful blog readers (and anyone who stumbles in by accident while innocently Googling *bricks and mortar* AND *graduated cylinders*): I never graduated from Kindergarten. That is an accomplishment that I cannot list on my CV; and since I have learned that Kindergarten graduation is a real thing, it has become an endless source of shame for me.

Oh, I went to Kindergarten. My teacher was an old woman named Mrs. T. How old she was I couldn't tell you because I was five at the time and she had gray hair so in my memory she was about a bajillion years old. I also remember that she wore bright red lipstick, often on her front teeth, and that she was a little bit scary.

Still, I probably learned a lot from her. We had those inflatable letter people in our classroom and a magic carpet to sit on for storytime. We were required to put together a lot of puzzles (and who knows what might have happened if we failed to complete that task) and write our letters just so. We fought over who got to play in the giant playhouse, and we drank a lot of milk. I even made a lifelong friend.

But I never graduated.

None of us did. I don't know if we were just the dumb class or what; but even though Mrs. T. sent us all on to muddle our way through the first grade, there were no graduation caps for us. No one played "Pomp and Circumstance." No one took video of us tugging at our itchy collars, tripping in our fancy shoes, or picking our noses right there in front of everybody.

But I guess my sad story has a happy ending because it is with a great deal of pride that I can report that both of my sons are first generation Kindergarten graduates. Just a few nights ago, I watched as my youngest son marched down the aisle of the high school auditorium, a mortarboard atop his little head, flash bulbs erupting all around him. I watched in awe as the Kindergarten class of 2013 stood and sang in (kind of) unison a parody of "New York, New York" ("I want to be a part of it: first grade, first grade…").

Okay, so it struck me as perhaps a tiny bit over the top when my son's name was called, and he marched across the stage to shake hands with the principal (he reached with his left because like most Kindergartners, he is more likely to hold hands than seal a business deal) and accept his diploma. I'm sure his Kindergarten degree will serve him well and earn him a much coveted position among the first grade classes of his hallowed elementary school.

Just maybe there was something important happening in that auditorium. Robert Fulghum might have been right when he wrote his famous essay, "All I Really Need to Know I Learned in Kindergarten." Kindergarteners learn to share and to play fair. They learn to be aware of what's around them, and they aspire to "live a balanced life — learn a little and draw and paint and sing and dance and play and work every day a little."

Most importantly, they start on a long educational journey, hopeful that the next big thing will be even better than what they have just worked so hard to complete. Kindergartners don their academic garb not as a celebration of completion, but as a promise of what is to come, a promise that someday they will learn proper nose-picking etiquette (we have to have a reason to celebrate middle school graduation). They wear their mortarboards with pride because nothing says, "Someday I'm going to be smarter than you," like absurd headwear.

A Hairy Tax Scheme: Ridding Society of Superfluous Burdens

As Englishman John Perry walked through the streets of Veronezh, Russia at the tail end of the 17th century, he encountered a man he had known for some time, but whom he hardly recognized. The man was a carpenter with whom Perry, an engineer who served in the court of Peter the Great, had worked before. For as long as Perry had known him, the carpenter, like most Russian men of the day, had worn a long beard and untrimmed mustache. Fresh from the barber, the carpenter now had a smooth face.

Perry exchanged a few pleasantries with the man and then asked what he had done with his beard. In response, the clean-cut carpenter pulled the beard from his breast pocket and explained that he would keep it some place safe, and that one day, it would be placed back upon his face in his coffin. That way, when he reached the pearly gates, St. Nicholas (who as we all know has a beard that's long and white) would know him.

The carpenter had become the latest victim of the tsar's

beard tax. Peter the Great had recently returned from what Wikipedia calls an "incognito" tour (meaning, I can only assume, that he wore a big, bushy, fake beard) through Europe in an attempt to drum up international support for his military campaign against the Ottoman Empire. His efforts failed (because obviously 17th-century Europeans hated beards), but Peter had learned his lesson; and on September 5, 1698, he issued a beard tax on the men of Russia (thus, essentially outlawing "No shave November").

And it was hefty, too. Wealthier citizens were required to pay 100 rubles per year (that's something like, well, a lot of rubles, I bet). The rest of the citizens had to pay a Copek (which is also probably a lot of Copeks) for the privilege of sporting a beard. In addition to the right to keep their whiskers (and incur the wrath of the tsar), payment of the tax also bought the unshaven a medallion they had to wear as proof of their legal right to bear registered whiskers. Evidently, concealing a beard inside your breast pocket did not require additional licensure.

The only men exempted from the law were the clergy who were allowed to maintain long beards and traditional dress, as the rest of the country embraced modern fashion trends. Even so, the clergymen were pretty hacked off about the whole thing and launched a pamphlet campaign, claiming that Peter (the Great Heretic) had gone much too far.

Like often happens with poorly handled calls to conservative ideals, the young men of Russia thumbed their noses at the outraged clergymen and happily got up early for work so they'd have time to shave every day. The real reason, of course, for the radical support of the misguided policies of the tsar was that the young ladies of Russia responded positively to the change.

I doubt such a tax would ever fly today, though, at least not here in the US where the beard has now taken on social icon status, and the men who wear them are far more likely to carry a duck call and a shotgun than to wear a medallion.

And I can't speak for all ladies, but for me personally, I don't mind so much. Now, I'm not a big fan of long, bushy facial hair; but a nicely trimmed beard tells me that while a man cares at least something for personal hygiene, he is also practical and confident enough to forego the daily ritual of shaving. I wouldn't want to begrudge him that option.

So I asked my husband (a handsome and neatly trimmed bearded fellow) what he thought about a beard tax. His anger at such a concept was as swift and unyielding as was that of the pamphlet-wielding Russian clergymen of old. I have to admit, the tax does seem remarkably unfair because men who wear beards already have to make great sacrifices in order to do so.

For example, this past weekend, when our family cooked out at the grandparents' house, we made s'mores, which we all enjoyed immensely. All, that is, except for my husband who, when questioned by our boys as to why he wasn't eating one of the gooey treats, replied by explaining that a bearded man must avoid melted marshmallow when he is far from his own shower.

Historians have suggested that the Russian beard tax was a part of Peter the Great's attempt to modernize (meaning Europeanize) his country, but there may have been a few practical advantages to the law as well. Regardless of his motive, Peter's tax was more or less successful. And it wasn't finally repealed until 1772, by which point John Perry's carpenter friend had probably long since carried his beard into Heaven.

September 12, 2013

The Completely Rational Fear of Triskaidekaphobia

On the morning of July 6, 1897, Captain William Fowler was discovered dead in his bed. According to those who knew him, Fowler was "in the best of health" when he retired the night before, but he evidently suffered a stroke and would never wake again. Of course, otherwise healthy or not, it could not have surprised many that Captain Fowler might suffer some bad luck.

Fowler was a man who laughed in the face of this world's truest dangers, and according to his obituary, he sure did live a dangerous life. As a boy, Fowler attended New York City's Public School No **13** until **13** years of age. After a brief stint in the printing industry, he became a builder who participated in the erection of **13** of the city's buildings.

On April **13**, 1861, Fowler took command of 100 (which is 7 x **13** + 9) Union volunteers, and over the course of nearly three years (only 10 less than **13**), participated in **13** major battles in the US Civil War (okay, that actually does sound fairly dangerous). Wounded, the captain was forced to resign his military position on August **13**, 1863. One month later, on September **13**, he bought the Knickerbocker Cottage on Sixth Avenue in New York, which he operated with his sons until finally selling it on Friday, April **13**, 1883.

Privately, Captain Fowler was a participating member of exactly **13** social and/or secret societies, including The **13** Club, which he founded on Friday, January **13**, 1882. His hope was that the group might dispel the popular notion that the number that had plagued him his entire life was inherently unlucky.

First on the list of superstitious beliefs to tackle was the notion that if **13** dined together, the first to rise from the table would die within a year's time. And so the group sat down together. Fortunately, none of these first diners did die within the year, and the society grew, continuing to meet at tables of **13** and adding new superstitions along the way.

At subsequent meetings, members entered the dining room (decorated with open umbrellas) by walking under a ladder, read from menus shaped like coffins, broke glasses with abandon, and carelessly spilled salt without throwing a single grain over their shoulders. We can assume that The **13** Club survived until the 1920s, when mentions of its meetings disappear from newspapers. Its membership at times swelled to as many as 400 people and allegedly included US presidents Arthur, Cleveland, Harrison, and Theodore Roosevelt.

I suspect that the fate-tempting activities of prominent men would not have inspired a great deal of confidence among the American population during what was a highly superstitious era. Recovering from a bloody civil war, the still relatively young United States was struggling to reinvent itself. As it tends to do, uncertainty bred superstition. And the efforts of Fowler's club didn't serve to assuage the public's fear, but the members certainly gave it a good try.

I suppose that is often the role of the well-educated and influential. At least that's what I am going to assume that my sons' school is playing at by placing the most dreadful day of the entire school calendar on Friday the **13**th. I'm speaking, of course, of school picture day, that annual nerve-wracking event that causes bad hair days, toothpaste spills, facial injury, and inevitable disappointment.

Maybe this wasn't your experience in school; but for me, no matter how long I spent gazing into the mirror to make sure I arrived at school unspoiled and looking as "okay" as I had it in me to look, sometime between the morning bell and picture line-up, disaster would strike. My hair got stringy (yes, that's probably the way it looked most of the time, but definitely not how it had looked in the mirror earlier that morning) and stuck out at odd angles; and my skin, which was perfectly clear only moments before, erupted in zits roughly the size and shape of Australia, and somehow I managed to get spinach in my teeth.

I guess it wasn't always *that* bad, but you get the idea. I actually don't know what I looked like in the sixth grade because there is no photographic evidence. I came home with the pictures, after refusing to show them to my friends, and told my mom (who isn't fond of having her picture taken) they were terrible and no one would ever see them. In the kind of awesome Mom moment that a grateful daughter (obviously) never forgets, my mom told me to throw them away. That's right. No updated photo for the grandparents. No wallet photos traded with friends.

If it hadn't been for the yearbook (curse it!), I would have gotten away completely clean. So at this point, I think it's only right to warn any readers out there who may have gone to grade school with me that if that picture were to resurface, my rage would be swift and my vengeance, terrible.

Even though I am not a particularly superstitious person (except as it applies to baseball fandom), I admit I am not above a little bit of anxiety at the thought of my boys heading to school to face a potentially emotionally scarring event on a day when many people still call in sick to work, just in case. I guess if the pictures don't turn out well, we can take advantage of retakes, which, I assume, will be scheduled for Friday, December **13**, exactly **13** weeks away. But now I'm just being silly.

After all, The **13** Club may not have risen from their tables of **13** only to be struck dead by a tour bus on the way home; but even Captain Fowler couldn't escape it when bad luck finally came calling for him, and he died peacefully in his sleep at the age of 69 (only 4 years beyond the age of **13** x 5), a mere 5 weeks and 3 days prior to Friday, August **13**, 1897. That can't just be a coincidence.

Have Bloomers. Will Travel.

In 1887, Thomas Stevens became the first man to circumnavigate the globe on a bicycle. A few years later, two wealthy Boston gentlemen became the first men to make an extravagant bet about whether or not a woman could perform a similar feat. It was an interesting question for the time. Could a woman, without exceptional means and without a male escort to protect her, rise to such an extreme physical challenge? The gentlemen needed only to find a woman who would be willing to try.

Annie Cohen Kopchovsky may not have seemed like a likely candidate. First of all, she was a young wife, responsible for three small children. Secondly, she had never ridden a bicycle. Still, no one could argue that Mrs. Kopchovsky had spunk. Convinced that anything a man could do, she most certainly could do, she volunteered for the trip. The rules of the bet stipulated that she must make stops in several specific world cities, complete the trip in just fifteen months (it had taken Stevens three years), begin the journey penniless, and through sponsorship raise $5,000 above her expenses.

Ms. Kopchovsky was well up to the task. First, she got herself an endorsement deal. The Londonderry Lithia Spring

Water Company provided her with $100, and she agreed to carry a placard for them and to ride under the name "Annie Londonderry." Then a few days before her scheduled departure, she took a bicycle riding lesson or two. I might have done that in the other order, but then I don't have Ms. Londonderry's spunk.

With only her placard (and I'm hoping some bottles of Londonderry), a change of clothes, and a pearl handled revolver, she started out on June 25, 1894, for the first leg of her journey, from Boston to Chicago.

By the time she reached Chicago, Londonderry had learned a few things. For one, she decided it made more sense to travel the other direction. Also, it was around this time that she traded in her skirts for bloomers (hopefully with padded spandex underneath) and her cumbersome 42-pound bicycle for a sleeker 21-pound men's bike. She then headed to New York where she left for France (by boat of course, though perhaps she participated in a few spinning classes while on board the ship).

After riding though France, Londonderry hopped a steamer to Egypt. From there, she travelled to Yemen and on to Sri Lanka and Singapore. After making mandatory appearances in China and Japan, she returned to the US at San Francisco, riding next to LA, El Paso, north to Denver, and finally finishing up in Chicago on September 23, 1895, one day shy of fifteen months. Along the way, Ms. Londonderry accumulated sponsorships and was cheered by enthusiastic supporters. Surviving injury and at times danger, Ms. Londonderry proved that a woman alone in a man's world could rise to whatever challenge she took in mind.

Now if you've followed this blog for very long, you've perhaps read a number of posts about bicycles. I assure you that this has far more to do with the historical significance of that particular vehicle than it does with my enthusiasm (which is genuine, but at best, sporadic) for the sport. In the late 19th century, the bicycle was much more than a great way to get some exercise. It was the impetus for the introduction of paved roadways in the US, so that when a pair of bicycle manufacturing brothers (Frank and Charles Duryea) invented the automobile, there was some place to drive it. Another pair of brothers in the bicycle business (Orville and Wilbur Wright) would eventually help us tame the skies as well.

And thanks to some spunky ladies, including Annie "Londonderry" Kopchovsky, the bicycle also offered women a freedom that few other things before it had. Shortly after Kopchovsky's journey, Susan B. Anthony famously said: "Let me tell you what I think of bicycling. I think it has done more to emancipate women than anything else in the world...I stand and rejoice every time I see a woman ride by on a wheel...the picture of free, untrammeled womanhood."

There's no question that American women of today have a great deal more freedom and opportunity than our ancestors once did, and I've been particularly blessed to be surrounded by strong women my whole life (and thankfully, many supportive strong men as well). One of the many strong women in my life is my big sister who just this past week completed her 2013 goal of riding 2013 miles on her bicycle.

She posted her success on Facebook, adding that by completing her "bike the year" goal for the fourth year in a row, she had biked more than 8000 miles over the past four years. I don't know about you, but I'm kind of tired just typing that. And especially when I consider that her mileage represents about a third of the way around the entire world.

To put this even further into perspective for myself, I rode my bike as part of my preparation for this post (if I were a more thorough and less practical historian, I would have worn bloomers), which brings my grand total up to somewhere around 70 miles for the year so far. Turns out, I'm not as spunky as my sister either.

Now if you do the math (and if you don't believe me, then you'll have to because I haven't shown my work), then you'll realize that Ms. Londonderry rode her bike approximately

18,580 miles. That's technically 6,321 miles short of the circumference of the earth. But if we assume participation in a couple of spinning classes, then I'd be willing to throw in a few more for that and call it good.

Still, if you feel the need to cry foul, you wouldn't be alone. Many of Ms. Londonberry's contemporaries accused her of traveling with a bike more than she traveled on one, and I will be happy to field your complaints just as soon as you log 18, 580 miles on your bicycle.

As for my sister, I certainly wouldn't bet against her if she said she was going to spend the next fifteen months circumnavigating the globe on her bicycle. But thanks to the legacy of some spunky ladies, she has lots of opportunities to show her strength in other ways as well. I guess a third of the way around the world in four years will do for now.

October 24, 2013

Terrorizing the Cat and Other Stupid Ways to Celebrate Your Birthday

A few weeks ago, I celebrated my 36th birthday. It was a pretty quiet affair. My husband was out of town for work about a week leading up to it, so he didn't have a lot of time for planning anything too special. He did take me out to dinner, though, and my sister baked me a cake the weekend before. And most importantly, I got so many sweet homemade cards from my boys. It was kind of perfect actually.

Because there's nothing particularly special about 36 (unless you're a mathematician that geeks out about perfect squares, I suppose), and I like keeping it low-key. I guess I could have done something spectacular to mark the day, like going to the casino to play roulette and wagering all the cash in my pocket (probably somewhere in the neighborhood of $5) on black, conquering my fear of public karaoke, or getting a tattoo on my back of a misspelled motivational saying.

Or I could have celebrated my birthday the way Annie Edson Taylor chose to spend her 63rd on October 24, 1901, when she became the first person ever (and yes, there have been others since) to go over Niagara Falls in a barrel.

Taylor had not had a great deal of good fortune in her lifetime. Born in 1838, she studied to be a teacher before meeting and marrying David Taylor. But marital bliss was not to be hers for long. He died shortly after the death of the couple's infant son. The young widow set out to make a life for herself and bounced around from job to job across the country, eventually meeting up with a girlfriend with whom she traveled to Mexico City (where presumably she got a tattoo: **DREAM AS IF YOU'LL LIFE FOREVER**).

Whatever she really did in Mexico City, Annie did not manage to find work; and so she made her way back north to Bay City, Michigan, where she had once briefly run a school for dance. It was there that she realized the best way for her to gain the means to support herself in comfort was to go to Niagara Falls and literally take the plunge.

Taylor got herself an agent and had a special barrel built. Then she did what any reasonable person would do. A couple of days before the planned stunt, she stuffed a cat into the barrel and sent it over the falls. The cat survived the trip with only a cut on its head (and an intense fear of being stuffed into a barrel) to show for it.

Apparently, that was a good enough result for Taylor; so two days later, she celebrated her 63rd birthday by allowing herself to be stuffed into the cushioned barrel, along with an extra pillow (you know, to make it comfortable).

The stunt itself took about twenty minutes, though reports say it took a little while to get the barrel open (during which time, I think it's safe to assume, Taylor developed an intense fear of being stuffed into a barrel). When it was finally opened, Taylor climbed out unharmed except for a minor gash on her head.

Of her experience, Mrs. Taylor had this to say:

> *If it was with my dying breath, I would caution anyone against attempting the feat… I would sooner walk up to the*

mouth of a cannon, knowing it was going to blow me to pieces than make another trip over the Fall.

Sadly, the whole fame and fortune plan didn't work out all that well for the daredevil. It turns out her agent was a crook, and Taylor died poor at the age of 82. Still, I would be lying if I said a (very small) part of me didn't admire Annie Taylor's pluck.

In fact, she has inspired me. Maybe, just maybe on my 63rd birthday, I will get myself a tattoo. I'm thinking: "**DON'T GO CHASING WATER**FLAWS."

November 14, 2013

Why You Should Have Smarter Friends and a Fabulous Cupcake Recipe

I spent this past Friday night in the company of friends and family, proving that I, a relatively informed and somewhat knowledgeable person, am, in fact, incredibly stupid. That's right, I attended a trivia night. I would say I *competed* in a trivia night, but that just wouldn't ring true.

Now it has come to my attention after living on the West Coast for a while and talking with folks who have lived in other parts of the US, that "Trivia Night" is somewhat regional. So let me give you a quick rundown in case you're not from around here.

Trivia nights are set up as fundraisers for, well, any kind of organization that might need to raise funds, like PTA, scouts, or even a local political party office. The one we attended was for a church youth program. To participate, you purchase a table and call up to seven of your quirkiest friends. The well-read guy, the film buff, the sports expert, and that one girl who can rattle off an exhaustive list of famous circus performers of the 19th century might be a good place to start.

It might also be wise to invite the friend who will supply the best snacks. It turns out that the only reason to call up your friend the practical historian is because she'll bring cupcakes.

Typically, there are ten questions in each of ten themed rounds. The top scoring two or three tables at the end of the evening are awarded a cash prize. These fundraising events have swept through the Midwest the last several years (so take *that*, all you trendsetting coastal cities), even sometimes inspiring traveling teams of trivia junkies (which you can be sure will include an expert on 19th century circus performers) that spend every weekend raiding the KC halls of sleepy little farm towns, making sure those of us with lives go home with nothing more than a few extra cupcakes.

In its earliest uses, the word "trivia" or the singular *trivium* referred in Ancient Rome to a coming together of three roads. Later, it referred to the *Artes Liberales*, the studies of grammar, rhetoric, and logic that form the basic learning that is important for all students (which is why college freshman still have to suffer through rhetoric & comp).

It wasn't until the 20th century that the term was applied consistently to bits of information that are of very little importance to the majority of the population. With the emergence of television came the rapid rise of the trivia game show. And though trivia on television nearly disappeared after it was revealed that the results of several of the games were fixed, the US had been bitten by the trivia bug.

College quiz bowls popped up across the country, started by Columbia University students Ed Goodgold and Dan Carklinsky whose book *Trivia* became a *New York Times* bestseller; probably because even though it had nothing to do with grammar, rhetoric, or logic, I'm guessing there was an entire chapter devoted to famous circus performers of the 19th century.

The 1980s brought us *Trivial Pursuit*, arguably the most popular board game of all time, and a second, much more successful run at the game show *Jeopardy!*, now the longest running game show in television history. So really the rapid growth in popularity of trivia night (one day soon, it may even reach culturally starved places like New York and Los Angeles) shouldn't come as much of a surprise.

Because every now and then, we all like to think of ourselves as relatively informed, somewhat knowledgeable people, and frankly, we need to be taken down a peg or two. So in our arrogance, we recruit our friends and put together teams to subject ourselves to questioning in categories such as: "Identification of State Capitol Buildings from Aerial Photographs," "Nominees who Failed to Win the Oscar for Best Supporting Actor in the 1930s," and "The Life and Times of 19th Century Circus Performers."

Then we wonder how on earth the team at the far end of the room that is averaging a score of 8 on every round has managed to sneak their smartphones past the judges. We'd probably say something about it, but our mouths are full of cupcake.

The Iceman's Custom Kicks

Shoelaces have lately been a source of great anxiety in our home. My six-year-old has been struggling to tie his shoes, working on it for months, in fact. He's a bit of a perfectionist, you see, and he doesn't respond well to instruction from his parents (fortunately he does much better with his school teachers). In the midst of our rushed mornings, I have been slowing down enough to (mostly) patiently show him the knot over and over, gently guide his fingers when he would allow me to, and encourage him along to my absolute wit's end.

We could just get him Velcro shoes and call it good, but I know this is a life skill he needs to have. It's just not intuitive for him, maybe not for people in general. Shoes used to be fastened with buckles, after all, and shoelaces weren't even invented until the end of the 18th century. At least, that's what I thought until I came across a story.

A little over 5000 years ago, a man named Ötzi tied his shoes and went for a walk through the Alps. Having forgotten to check his weather app before leaving, the forty-something-year-old shepherd got caught in a sudden winter storm and unfortunately died of exposure. But don't feel too bad for him because he just as likely died from blood loss after receiving an arrow wound to the shoulder. And he might have been with several friends at the time, which means it's possible that his walk was really a raid of some sort. What we do know is that Ötzi was almost certainly not his real name.

This "Ötzi" is Europe's oldest natural mummy, dating to about 3,300 BC, and discovered in 1991 in the Ötzal Alps on the Austria/Italy border. Much of this ancient gentleman's story is speculation, of course, but it amazes me how much is known about him. For example, scientists know that Ötzi was lactose intolerant, was likely sterile, and that he had a two-week bout of illness about two months before he died.

But despite these challenges, Ötzi had an unwavering sense of style. The mummy was found wearing a full set of clothing, including leggings, loincloth, coat, belt, and a hat, all sewn from leathers of various animal skins. He also sported a great pair of shoes.

It's his shoes that interest me the most because for a while, they were the oldest leather shoes that archaeologists had ever discovered. And they had laces. There are some older, fibrous sandals dating back about 8000 years that were discovered in the 1950s in caves in my own great state (because what Missourian doesn't love a great pair of shoes). And a few years after the discovery of Ötzi the Ice Man, several pairs of slightly older leather laced shoes were discovered in an Armenian cave.

The cool thing about all of the shoe discoveries is that even though we have pretty good anatomical evidence that people have been wearing them for around 40,000 years, shoes tend to be made from materials that don't preserve all that well. And because of the laced-up design of both Ötzi's shoes and the cave shoes, we now know that when the Englishman Harvey Kennedy patented the shoelace back in 1790, he was really just standing on the shoulders of ancient giants in the shoe industry.

Humans have been tying shoes and tripping on trailing

laces for millennia. And it's possible that for as long as there have been shoes to tie, there have been trends in fashion footwear to follow. According to archaeologist Jacqui Wood who has studied both footwear discoveries, "The Iceman's shoe was in another league altogether."

The Armenian shoes are of a simpler design that has been seen over a long period of time in different parts of the world. It was the everyman's shoe design. Ötzi, however, had himself a custom pair of kicks with the sides and bases made of different types of leather and netting on the inside to pull the shoes tight around the foot.

You can bet that when Ötzi laced up his shoes in the morning, it was with great pride, probably using something fancy like a surgeon's knot or a turquoise turtle shoelace knot. Or maybe he went for speed using the standard Ian knot, which claims to be the fastest shoelace knot in the world.

Personally, I like the traditional loop, swoop, and pull method, and that's the one I have been attempting to teach to my son. Though he's been able to hit a thrown baseball since he was three and has an unbelievable natural tennis swing (which I think is safe to say he did NOT inherit from his mother), his fine motor skills have been a little slower to develop. So when yesterday morning he finally tied his shoes entirely by himself, this mama was ready to celebrate.

Of course, my husband recently injured the ulnar collateral ligament in his dominant thumb and is now wearing a brace that makes shoe tying virtually impossible, so I still have to tie someone else's shoes in the morning. Alas, a mother's work is never done.

December 5, 2013

On Dasher, on Dancer, on Prancer, on Vixen, on Dominick, on Snoopy, on Baron von Richthofen

It's beginning to look a lot like Christmas here in the Angleton home. As is tradition for our family, we decorated the tree the day after Thanksgiving (alas, I missed out on all the Black Friday deals), and the Christmas geese are shining brightly in the front yard.

It's also beginning to sound an awful lot like Christmas, as it has become our new tradition to crank up the volume on the Christmas iTunes list to sing and dance our way through dinner prep and homework in the evenings. My six-year-old has taken to shuffling through the songs to find what he most wants to hear, which means that we skip over Bing Crosby's "White Christmas" and instead listen to Lou Monte's "Dominick the Donkey" A LOT. It also means that homework is taking a little longer these days.

But I can't complain too much because even though there

are some great songs we're missing out on, the kid has some pretty good taste. One that he has been particularly enjoying is The Royal Guardsmen's 1967 "Snoopy's Christmas."

Both of my boys like this one, which makes a practical historian mama proud because the song indirectly honors what has to be one of my favorite moments in all of human history. It's a follow-up to "Snoopy vs. the Red Baron," a 1966 release that tells the tale of Charles Schultz's lovable cartoon beagle who in October of 1965 began fantasizing about engaging the WW I German flying ace often known as the Red Baron in a dogfight.

The Red Baron's real name was Manfred von Richthofen. He emerged from the defunct cavalry division of the German Imperial Army to train as a pilot, apparently with a fair amount of natural talent. With nearly 80 confirmed kills and most likely over 100 in all, he was the most successful fighter pilot of the war, becoming something of a legend to both sides of the struggle.

Of course because he is such a legendary figure, there is some controversy surrounding his eventual death. Richthofen was wounded and went down (remarkably gracefully, according to reports) over France on April 21, 1918. He died from the shot to his chest, moments after landing. The trouble is that it has proven difficult to know who shot him.

The kill was long credited to Canadian pilot Captain Arthur Brown, but there is a good deal of evidence that the fatal shot came from the ground. Several historians have assigned credit to various anti-aircraft gunners who were in the area at the time. Still, others believe that it was in fact Snoopy perched atop his flying doghouse that drove the Baron to the ground, where he survived the wound and went on to start a highly successful frozen pizza business.

The problem with that last theory is that if we assume a certain degree of historical accuracy in the well-researched work of The Royal Guardsmen, then Snoopy and the Red Baron met one more time, on Christmas Eve.

This encounter ended very differently than the first. The Red Baron had Snoopy in his sights and instead of moving in for the kill, forced him to the ground for a friendly Christmas toast, after which the two parted ways peacefully.

I regret to inform you that there is no record of this encounter in the history books nor of a similar one involving Richthofen; but there is a truly wonderful occasion documented in the history of WW I on which primarily British and German troops fighting in the trenches of the Western Front called a spontaneous truce and celebrated together on Christmas of 1914.

Accounts describe German soldiers beginning to sing carols on Christmas Eve and placing small, lighted trees along the edge of the trenches. Soon makeshift signs expressing Christmas greetings and suggesting a temporary peace appeared on both sides; and by morning, soldiers emerged to cross no-man's land and shake hands. All day (and according to some accounts, for several after) soldiers took time to bury fallen comrades, exchange small gifts, and even play football (soccer) together.

This "Christmas Truce" was not government sanctioned and in fact followed a flat rejection on both sides of a December 7th suggestion from Pope Benedict XV that a temporary ceasefire be declared in honor of the holiday. Of course, eventually the fighting started again and the war raged on for four more bloody years.

Never again in World War I, nor in any conflict since, has a similar truce been effectively carried out; but for one brief shining moment in history, the commonality of basic humanity triumphed over the absurdity of war. And Snoopy and the Red Baron shared a Christmas toast. I think that's something worth singing about, even if it means I can't always dream of a white Christmas as much as I'd like.

December 19, 2013

"Hey, Mom! Do you think this would blow up if I...?"

In 1878 Bishop Milton Wright, who traveled frequently in his work for the Church of the United Brethren in Christ, brought home a gift for his two youngest sons. Milton and his wife Susan, who in truth was much more mechanically minded than him, liked to encourage their children's inquisitiveness and creativity because that's the kind of parents they were. The gift seemed to be just the right kind of thing.

What he brought was a propeller toy based on the models designed by Frenchman Alphonse Pénaud. It was constructed with paper, bamboo, and cork and powered by a wound rubber band. Milton's young sons, Wilbur and Orville Wright, played with the toy again and again until it broke. Then they made another one themselves.

Years later, when the brothers' innovations led to the first sustainable flight fixed-wing aircraft, they traced their interest in flight back to the propeller toy their father had given them when they were about six and ten years old.

Because that's the kind of dad he was.

A few years later, when younger brother Orville was nine, he wrote a letter to his father who was once again away on church business:

Dear Father,

My teacher said I was a good boy today. We have 45 in our room. The other day I took a machine can and filled it with water. Then I put it on the stove. I waited a little while and the water came squirting out of the top about a foot. The water in the river was up in the cracker factory about half a foot. There is a good deal water on the island. The old cat is dead.

Your son Orville

I love that amidst the obligatory behavior report (a bit of a troublemaker, Orville was once expelled from an elementary school for poor behavior), details about local water levels, and the reported death of a family pet, there is this irresponsible and dangerous experiment bursting from the page. I love this letter because as the mother of a couple inquisitive and creative kids, I find it wonderfully familiar.

My oldest son will soon turn nine, and this sounds so much like him. Of course, his "letter" would be more likely to arrive in my inbox as a power point presentation and/or short movie detailing the latest way he has risked his safety in the name of science. Because that's just the kind of kid he is.

But it's the same idea. I imagine this letter made Milton Wright smile because he probably suspected that his kids would grow up to do amazing things. And because there's no greater moment in parenthood than when your kids want to share their enthusiasm with you.

As I watch my little mister blow out the nine candles on his birthday cake, I will have a few wishes of my own to make. My wish is that he will continue to be an inquisitive kid who delights in creativity and that I will be the kind of parent who encourages him along the way. I wish to always be one of the people he can't wait to tell about his latest discovery.

And I wish to someday watch him take flight.

A Good Old Fashioned Spellen Thraw Doun

In 1913, a congressman from Ohio named Frank B. Willis became the greatest speller in the United States. That's because the National Press Club, begun in 1908, had thrown down the gauntlet, challenging politicians to what it called an "old fashioned spelling bee."

The Scripps National Spelling Bee that we all watch with bated breath on ESPN (because well, I don't know, I guess there's just something irresistible about watching a twelve year old spell words we're pretty sure don't really exist) didn't start until 1925. So just how "old fashioned" the press vs. politician spelling throw down was gets a little difficult to pinpoint.

The term "spelling bee" cropped up around 1850, and probably has more to do with a social event such as a "quilting bee," where people come together to bestow a favor, rather than from the industrious little insects that pollinate the world's fruit trees. And we know that there were "trials in spelling," "spelling matches," and "spelling flights" as early as the late 1700s, with Benjamin Franklin getting in on the action by promoting the usefulness of such activities in schools.

Some have even attempted to trace the spelling bee back to Shakespeare's day, quoting a passage from *The English Schoole-Maister* by Edmund Coote in which a pair of students debates the importance of particular letters in the spelling of the word "people". I'm not sure I buy that connection totally, but there is, I think, a lesson from the Elizabethan era that may point to why spelling bees developed.

Because as everyone who has ever taken an English class in which he or she had to read Shakespeare, or write an essay, or take a spelling test knows, English is kind of a stupid language. Now I mean that with the greatest possible respect because English is, after all, my native language, and certainly the only one I speak with much confidence (if it wasn't so sad, my Spanish would be hilarious). But it wasn't until the late 1500s that English spelling was all that well standardized, as anyone who has ever taken a Chaucer class can tol ye.

I guess what I'm saying is that learning to read and write in a language that has lots of rules that it rarely follows can be a little frustrating. This, probably more than any other factor, must have led to the development of the spelling bee because just like correctly identifying ad slogans from the 1950s at the local pub trivia night, knowing how to correctly spell onomatopoeia gives you bragging rights in my book.

So I was pleased to attend the school-wide spelling bee at my oldest son's school this week. He was the champion representing his third grade classroom, one of probably about 20 or so kids in the final competition that included 3rd through 5th graders. Not to brag or anything (meaning that I'm totally going to brag), but E is a voracious reader, a great speller, and he won his second grade bee last year against 20 or so of the finest spellers the primary school had to offer.

I probably don't have to tell you he was a little nervous, and that I was possibly even more nervous. Logically, I knew that he was unlikely to win as a third grader, and it was important to me that he understood my expectations were only for him to relax and do his best. I was pretty worried that if he was eliminated early, he would be inconsolably upset.

Sitting among the crowd of anxious parents, I realized we all had that same fear. With every mistake, each parent winced, our hearts beating a little faster as we waited to see whether the eliminated kiddo would burst into tears. Many of them did.

Fortunately, E lasted until only two rounds before the champion was crowned, and by then, he had outperformed several older kids. Even though he lost because he second-guessed himself on a word we had practiced the night before, he was pleased with how well he had done. And I have never been prouder of him.

Because English is stupid. And spelling it is hard. But learning to lose graciously and move on is one of the most difficult lessons everyone eventually has to learn.

The National Press Club (a group of people who write in English professionally) had to learn that lesson in 1913 when a congressman from Ohio, a former professor of history and economics, schooled them.

They got their chance for redemption this past September when the National Press Club hosted a Centennial Spelling Bee throw down as a fundraiser for the nonprofit Journalism Institute. This time, it was Senator Tim Kaine of Virginia that claimed the victory over all the teary-eyed members of the press.

The Legacy of Two Pies

Ivan

It's 1° F outside according to my thermometer, and weather.com tells me that the wind chill is a frigid -13° F. So I guess I can understand why we got that dreaded phone call this morning, just after 5 AM, announcing that there would be no school today. At these temperatures, our busses, stored outdoors, don't like to start, and it's just too cold for even well-bundled kiddos to wait outside for them anyway.

Still, we've now missed seven days of school since winter break (the same number of days we've had school), and my boys are even starting to be genuinely disappointed when the phone rings in the morning.

Which leaves me with a big task of trying to find ways of entertaining them. But at least for today, I think I have it covered because I found an obscure holiday for us to celebrate. It just so happens that today is National Pie Day.

First, it's important to distinguish this from *Pi* Day, which celebrates everyone's favorite irrational number on March 14 (3/14 in the US). Though the holidays are celebrated similarly, the January 23rd holiday is sponsored by the American Pie Council (without whom there would be no one to tell us that pie is pretty tasty) as opposed to fun-loving math nerds (without whom there would be no one to, well, pretty much make our modern world function).

But this is more than just a day for the American Pie Council to promote its controversial agenda (that we should all eat more pie). Though the holiday as we know it today got started in 1986 to commemorate the 75th anniversary of Crisco, the roots of National Pie Day actually reach much further than that.

It all started with a Bulgarian hermit named Ivan Rilski born in about 880 in what is today the city of Sophia. Saint Ivan made his home in the wilderness of the Rila Mountains, where he became known as a healer who dodged fame whenever possible, even spurning a visit from Bulgaria's Tsar Peter I.

Still disciples came and soon formed the Rila Monastery that today is the largest and most visited Eastern Orthodox monastery in Bulgaria. There are many miracles associated with St. Ivan, most involving healing, but also quite a few involving feeding the hungry. For a time, St. Ivan is said to have sustained himself and visitors on beans provided by God in the wilderness; but when others attempted to remove them from his presence, they found that the beans had vanished.

And there's another story involving a rare visit to a nearby village in which St. Ivan, himself the very picture of self-denial and reliance upon God, arrived at the homes of his hungry neighbors bearing two pies. The story earned the saint the nickname "Two Pies Ivan," but as I have been able to find it, it is maddeningly short on details.

Allegedly, Saint Ivan got the pies from the local pie maker, and they were his last two. The event is referred to as a miracle, but it is admittedly unclear to me exactly why. Perhaps two pies would have been insufficient to feed the crowd of hungry villagers, and there was a miraculous multiplication, such as in the case of the loaves and fishes of the New Testament. Or perhaps Saint Ivan simply used a bit of Jedi mind trickery to solicit a pie donation from the local pie maker.

Really, I think, though, that if a strange, old hermit who is known to barely subsistence-live in the mountains shows up on your doorstep with two pies, it might just seem like something of a miracle.

Whatever happened, it's clear that St. Ivan showed up in the right place at the right time, bearing just the right gifts. His example of faith earned him the title of Patron Saint of Bulgaria and also Patron Saint of pies and pie makers.

And so nearly a month and a half before we bake a pie to celebrate *pi* day, we bake TWO pies to celebrate the legacy of Two Pies Ivan. The American Pie Council encourages trying new pie recipes on this day and also sharing pie with your neighbors. That sounds like a pretty good idea to me. My neighbors are probably having a rough day because I hear the wind chill is -13° F, and their kids are stuck at home. I imagine if a neighbor in a similar situation shows up at their door bearing pie, it might seem like something of a miracle.

February 20, 2014

Puppy Love and the Harbinger of Death

In 1898, *The Connecticut Quarterly* included an essay entitled "The Black Dog." Written by geologist W. H. C. Pynchon and printed not long after his mysterious death, the essay relates the story of a possibly otherworldly dog that is said to haunt the Hanging Hills region that overlooks the town of Meriden in Connecticut.

According to local lore, the dog appears to travelers on the mountains up to three times. The first sighting brings joy; the second, misery; and the third, death. The Hanging Hills tale is not entirely unique, of course. Dating back to at least the early 12th-century, beastly black hounds have portended death throughout the English countryside.

Sir Arthur Conan Doyle featured the devilish dog in *The Hound of Baskervilles*, but the legend is much older than that, showing up in literature and eye witness accounts, not to mention it has long held a certain fascination for students of divination at Hogwarts School of Witchcraft & Wizardry.

But old Black Shuck, as he is often known, really isn't in the same league as the little animal in Pynchon's essay. He describes the beast not as a huge ghostly monster with glowing red eyes but as a plain old dog the shade of "an old

black hat that has been soaked in the rain a good many times."
Pynchon's dog is friendly, playful even, and of "uncertain
lineage."

To be fair, Pynchon does describe the dog as making no
sound when it barks, nor footprints when it walks. Still, it's
otherwise basically just a sweet, little ole mutt, not unlike the
puppy that has recently taken up residence in my home.

I don't exactly consider myself a "dog person;" and
although my family had a dog when I was a child and I
endured a brief stint as a professional dog trainer just after
college, I've never had a strong desire for the responsibility of
owning one myself. But my sons are six and nine now, and (as
everyone keeps telling me) a boy needs a dog.

Since most of the time nothing good comes of social
media, my husband and I fell victim to adorable pictures of
puppies who needed good homes after my cousin's
kindhearted neighbor took in an abandoned mama dog that
promptly gave birth to *eleven pups.*

Because even if you're not a classic "dog person," there's
no denying that the critters can worm their way into your
heart pretty fast. That happened to Pynchon as well. On his
first journey into the Hanging Hills region in the spring of
1889, the dog saw him and accompanied him along the way.
When the animal disappeared at the end of the return journey,
Pynchon was a little sad that he'd lost such a good
companion.

Three years later, Pynchon returned to the area, this time
accompanied by fellow geologist Herbert Marshall who
laughed about having seen the legendary mutt two times
previously, but doubting that he might really be in any serious
danger. After the men encountered the dog on their journey
and Marshall almost immediately fell into a ravine and died,
Pynchon was a believer.

Six years would pass before his duties with the Geological
Survey would take him back to Hanging Hills. This time, he
journeyed alone and never returned. His body was later

recovered in the same ravine in which Marshall had died.

I am something of a skeptic when it comes to cryptozoology, and I suppose demon ghost dogs that portend death fit into that category. Pynchon seems like a reliable enough witness, but the suggestion of local lore and hiking through the mountains can do crazy things to your psyche.

Of course, I've also admitted that I'm not much of a *dog person*; and yet, I now live with a playful little black puppy named Ozzie, and he brings me a lot of joy. It's also true that when he poops on my carpet he provides me with a little bit of misery; and if he doesn't learn to sleep through the night, he may yet be the death of me.

Why Bricklaying is the Devil's Work

I confess I'm a sucker for a good treasure hunt. I love the idea of solving riddles, breaking codes, and following the winding path through an unfolding conspiracy. I cheer as the ever expressionless Nicholas Cage blazes through hundreds of years of US history, as Tom Hanks discovers long-unnoticed symbols on the world's most revered and well-studied works of art, and as Harrison Ford stands before an ancient knight and chooses wisely.

And my heart delights in exploring the fictional possibilities provided by the secret societies that make such plots possible, all of which seem to somehow relate to the Freemasons.

I wish I could give you a concise history of them because they are fascinating. Unfortunately, there's not a lot known (at least by outsiders) about the origin of the Freemasons. I mean, sure, there is a circle of thirteen Grand Masters who each have a part of a code leading to a series of clues (39 in all) throughout the world that when put together will reveal the secret history of the fraternity and simultaneously signal the apocalypse. Probably.

Outside of that, what I have been able to uncover (in a

brief Internet search) is that there are people who have spent A LOT longer searching through MUCH more reliable sources and have come up with some thoughts.

Basically, the Freemasons most likely started as actual stonemasons. Or they were influenced by actual stonemasons. And though there have been attempts to trace the group back to the pyramid builders of Ancient Egypt and to Solomon's temple, all we really know is that documentation suggests it may have developed sometime before 1400.

Whether the organization formed from a trade guild of masons finding that they already had a structure in place that might serve to make the world a better place, or whether the first Freemasons were regular guys who wanted to do all of those things and thought the allegory of the tools used by literal builders was pretty neat, is anyone's guess. Either way, the fraternity has long existed for the purpose of promoting the dignity of the individual, the right to freedom of religious worship, the need for public education, and the establishment of democracy.

Or so they claim.

But because we all know that conspiracy theorists and Hollywood screenwriters are generally good sources of reliable information, I think it's safe to say that Freemasons are really just a group of powerful satanic treasure-hoarders who are plotting to take over the world to the tune of $1.5 million in charitable contributions per day.

Clearly, Freemasonry has done and is doing some great things in the world. Still, it has run into its share of serious criticism from major world religions that find within its devotion to ritual and secrecy the components of a religion itself, one that may in many ways conflict with mainstream Christian, Jewish, and Islamic teachings.

I won't pretend to be an expert on Freemasonry and its relationship to world religions, but I will say that I am convinced that masonry is the devil's work.

I say this because late this past Saturday afternoon, my

husband was looking at a flower bed at the corner of our house, and he made a rash decision. Our lot is pretty hilly, and so this flower bed is the height of a single landscape block on one end, but becomes a four foot retaining wall at the corner of the house. And it's been falling.

So, my husband, who is *not* a mason by trade, decided that Saturday afternoon was the right time for him to transform into an "expert" bricklayer, removing the heavy stones and laying them all over our yard, so he could rebuild the wall, level and perfect. He did not look at a forecast first.

So then when Saturday evening brought him news of a family emergency and with it, plans to be out of town the next day; and with the first part of the week promising rain to wash away all of the exposed dirt pile in our corner flowerbed, it fell to me (also *not* a mason by trade) to build a brick wall.

Here's the thing. I get bricks. I played with LEGO blocks as a kid. And I watched my husband tamp down the dirt, lay the paver gravel, and check several times with the level before laying the block and checking it again. I had even helped out by handing him tools. How hard could it be, right?

And it's not that hard to lay the blocks on top of one another once that first layer is level, but I was working on a slope so there were still quite a few blocks that needed to be placed directly on the ground itself. After an hour or so, I had gotten to the point that I could lay a level brick on the dirt after several attempts. And then I got to a brick that had to lay half on the dirt and half on another brick.

It took me three hours. THREE. HOURS. For one brick. ONE. BRICK. Neighbors stopped by to laugh ~~with~~ at me as I reveled in my incompetence. But I finally did it. Because I was determined to do it. It was a matter of pride. After my eventual success, I took a few pictures, put a tarp over the whole darn thing, and walked away.

Now I know that the average mason doesn't spend three hours to place one brick; at least if he does, I hope he doesn't charge by the hour. So the only conclusion that I can draw is that he must have sold his soul. And I have to assume that 15th century masons did as well.

Because that is the only way I can see them successfully building great architectural wonders in which they could hide clues leading to vast amounts of undiscovered wealth that would one day be rediscovered by nerdy treasure hunters seeking to return it to the world, thereby foiling the Freemason attempt at total world domination. Probably.

Strychnine, Stray Dogs, and Bad Apples: How Not to Host a Marathon

On August 30, 1904, the city of St. Louis hosted the third Olympic men's marathon. A relatively young sporting event, the marathon had been designed in order to pay homage to the Greek legend of Pheidippides and promoted as the flagship Olympic event in the first successful modern Olympic games of 1896.

Despite its brief history, the sport did attract a number of top athletes, many of whom did not attend the 1904 Olympic games. In all, there were thirty-two athletes who did participate, representing only four nations. Fourteen of the runners actually finished the race.

Of those, the winner used performance enhancing drugs *during* the race (well, okay, so it was strychnine; but at the time, it was considered performance enhancing). The fourth place finisher ate a couple of bad apples, got sick, and took a nap during the event. And one athlete was chased almost a mile off course by a stray dog.

But at least only one runner was disqualified for

completing a large part of the race in a car (the same man went on to win the Boston Marathon the next year. On foot).

Chicago had been the original choice to host; but because the Olympics would compete with the St. Louis World's Fair (of iced tea and waffle cone fame), the IOC agreed to move the games, so the events could be combined. In retrospect, it probably wasn't a great choice.

Not only were the games desperately overshadowed by the fair, but the 24.85 mile marathon course (the event wasn't standardized to 26 miles 385 yards until 1924) was filled with brutal hills, littered with road debris, and covered in so much dust that one runner collapsed from hemorrhaging after dust coated his esophagus and ripped his stomach lining. The event was begun in the late afternoon in the miserably hot and humid weather typical of St. Louis in August, and water was made available to the athletes in only two locations along the course. Frankly, it's a wonder any of them finished and lived to tell the tale.

But I am happy to report that since then, St. Louis has gotten quite a bit better at hosting marathons. This past weekend saw the city alive with many running events associated with the St. Louis Go! Marathon.

In its 14th year, the Go! is a weekend of family fitness activities, including fun runs for all ages and culminating in a half, full, and relay marathon event. Even better, the website insists that there are a full 17 water and Gatorade stations available along the route, so participants can comfortably skip the strychnine. The event attracts over 25,000 participants each year and is, in general, pretty darn cool.

Now, you may have gathered, as much as I appreciate physical fitness and enjoy staying in shape, I don't run. Well, unless I have to, which I rarely do. But I did attend the Saturday of Go! weekend to cheer on my oldest son, who participated this year in the Read, Right, & Run Go! Marathon.

This, to me, is probably the best run of the weekend because it is a celebration of six months of hard work for the grade K-5 participants. It's organized through area elementary schools that work to help students complete 26 acts of service, read 26 books, and run 26 miles in order to qualify for the final celebration run.

Over 6000 students representing 250 schools participated this year, which means that in the St. Louis area, little kids performed more than 156,000 good works, read more than 156,000 books, and ran more than 156,000 miles. And as far as I have been able to find, not a single one of those kids got sick from eating bad apples during the race or got chased off course by wild dogs.

So, go St. Louis! It may have taken a try or two to get it right, but it looks like you're a marathon city after all.

April 24, 2014

Three Legs are Better than Two

Despite my best efforts, it's been a crazy week here at our house. Before starting our family, now over nine years ago, my husband and I decided that we would try very hard not to be *that* family. You know the one.

Well, actually you might not know them very well. They are the neighbors that are never home. Instead, they're on the run because Sally has dance class at the same time that Billy has soccer practice; and Lulu has to get to her Girl Scout meeting, which starts at the same time as Freddie's trumpet lesson. By the time they do get home, they only have time to hope that everyone ate dinner at some point, crank out a little homework, brush their teeth, and get to bed, which they had better do quickly because they have a busy day tomorrow.

And most of the time, we are not *that* family. Or at least a lot of the time we're not. But, of course, sometimes we are. We're lucky, though, because in our family there are two parents and two children, which means that when the week gets a little hectic, we can still coordinate and run the race pretty well.

That is, until we get to a week when the baseball season is in full swing for our nine-year-old who is also preparing for a piano recital and just volunteered for a speaking role in the upcoming third grade musical. And tee-ball season has begun for our six-year-old who is also taking first Communion class and his pre-summer "Mom is concerned you might otherwise drown" refresher swim classes.

And Dad has work meetings almost every night of the week.

Oh, and we should probably all eat dinner at some point. Also, the boys have homework that they don't want to do because it's nice weather, and they'd rather play outside, and frankly, I'd rather let them. But I can't. Because I certainly don't want to be *that* mom.

On those weeks, when I'm running mostly alone, with two kids who are off in different directions, I begin to think that maybe I deserve a medal. Except that I really don't because I never feel like I can quite make it across the finish line in time, even though I am reasonably certain we've all eaten dinner at some point each evening this week.

I have to wonder if that's how US track star Lawson Robertson was feeling when he competed in the 13th annual championship tournament of the Military Athletic League held at Madison Square Garden in April of 1909. Robertson was coming off of a disappointing performance in the 100-meter sprint at the 1908 Olympics. Clocking 11.2 seconds in his semifinal heat, the same time as a fellow countryman who went on to compete in the final event, Robertson failed to advance by less than a foot.

Though he had earned a bronze medal in the standing high jump in 1904 and was a noted sprinter who would go on to coach for the US track & field teams in future Olympics, the Olympic sprinting medals eluded him. Still, there is one record for which he will always be known, a world record that has continued to stand for 105 years.

On April 24, 1909, Robertson teamed up with fellow American track & field star Harry Hillman (best known as a hurdler who claimed three Olympic gold medals in hurdling in 1904 and a silver in 1908) for the 100-yard (91-meter) three-legged race. The men clocked in at a never-since-equaled 11 seconds.

Admittedly, I'm not sure there have been many challenges to the record (assuming that the average Sunday school picnic doesn't count as official); but still, I like the idea that these two men, neither of whom achieved much success as individual record-breaking sprinters, combined forces and established possibly permanent dominance as partners in the world of competitive three-legged racing.

I suspect that Hillman and Robertson's race was somewhat more graceful than the average three-legged event. Probably even more graceful than the stumbling through a busy crazy week that my husband and I occasionally do, when we can no longer avoid being *that* family for a little while.

Still, I'm grateful that next week, when the third-grade musical is on the same night as the baseball game, scheduled just far enough apart that with a quick change in the car, we should be able to make both, I'll have my racing partner back. I'm betting I'm going to need him, but I haven't yet been brave enough to check next week's tee-ball practice schedule.

These Boots are NOT Made for Walking

On October 28, 1533, the 14-year-old Catherine de Medici married the Duke of Orleans, the second son of King Francis I of France. And a fine match it was, too. As a member of a powerful and wealthy Italian family, Catherine was orphaned at a young age and so became the sole heiress to a vast fortune. And though she was of relatively common birth, her mother had been the daughter of French nobility. Catherine was well-educated and had proven resilient as a political captive in Florence for several years.

But for all that recommended her, Catherine was, according to contemporary accounts, under five feet tall, had the "protruding eyes" of her family, and was "not pretty in the face." Anxious to make a good impression on her groom and his countrymen, she did what any sensible woman would do. She got herself a great pair of shoes.

Fortunately, her cobbler knew just what to do. He replaced the common wooden soles of Catherine's shoes with a narrow four-inch heel, making her appear taller and at the same time, lending her an alluringly awkward gait, bunchy calves, and intense foot pain. The people of France, who had never seen such fashionable footwear, were impressed. Henry of Orleans, who would one day be King Henry II of France, wasn't.

Alas, Catherine's marriage was not a particularly happy one, but it did signal the beginning of a terribly uncomfortable fashion trend that has waxed and waned through the centuries, never entirely going away.

Now, I'm a fairly practical woman, and I'm delighted that I don't work in a field in which high heels are a necessary part of my professional image. Most days will find me sporting my comfy tennis shoes; or perhaps now that the weather is warming up, my trusty Tevas that have survived ocean waves, river muck, and lots of sunny days at the park. But I admit that every once in a while I feel that pull to don a pair of stilettos.

A couple of weeks ago, I decided to do just that. We attended the wedding of one of my husband's longtime friends. As a member of the wedding party, my man was going to look pretty fancied up, so I thought I'd make an effort. I bought a new dress, and of course, some great shoes to match and give me the bunchy calves that would be nicely set off by my hemline.

To my utter delight, one of the first women I encountered, as we arrived at the country club where the wedding was to take place, remarked about how much she liked my shoes. I thanked her and commenced to help put the finishing touches around the patio area, where the wedding party and guests would stand to witness the happy couple's I dos.

It was a beautiful day, and the ceremony was sweet and intimate and perfect. But as I look back to how long I stood on a concrete patio in my heels, I do sort of question my sanity. When it was over and we'd danced our way through the reception and were finally climbing into the car at the end of the night, I kicked off the shoes and realized I had never in my life felt the kind of pain I then felt in my right foot.

When it still kind of hurt to walk a week later, I started thinking something might be wrong. It turns out, my fabulous shoes (and by extension, because I believe in putting blame where it belongs, Catherine de Medici) had given me a not-so-fabulous stress fracture. And apparently that really isn't all that unusual. In fact, though a stress fracture in the foot isn't quite as common among frequent high heel wearers as say corns, ingrown toenails, back pain, knee pain, and thickening of the Achilles tendon, it still happens. Often.

In 2003, the American Podiatric Medical Association conducted a survey and found that 42% of women admitted to wearing uncomfortable shoes for the sake of style. They also found that of the remaining 58% of survey participants, at least 2/3 were lying.

This has me wondering why we do this to ourselves. And also, whether or not I have learned my lesson. I think Catherine de Medici answered the first question almost 500 years ago. Her ridiculous shoes gave her the lift she needed to meet an intimidating situation in the eye, with the style and grace (and back pain) she would one day need as Queen Regent of France. The second question is harder to answer. If I had to guess today, I'd probably say I'll cautiously wear heels again. But then by the time I finish up six weeks clunking around in a remarkably less fashionable boot splint, I may have changed my mind.

May 22, 2014

Willy-Nilly from the Middle

In about 1892, a Connecticut dentist by the name of Dr. Lucius Sheffield traveled to Paris and observed the same artists who had recently protested the creation of a useless and monstrous tower diligently painting pictures of *la Tour Eiffel* to sell to useless and monstrous American tourists. It wasn't the works of art, however, that he admired, but rather it was the tubes from which the artists squeezed their paint.

You see, Lucius Sheffield was a second generation dentist, the son of Dr. Washington Sheffield, famous for the 1850 invention of modern toothpaste and the founder of the Sheffield Dentrifice Company. The Sheffield "Crème Dentifrice" was said to "[arrest] decay, [check] infection and [keep] the oral cavity sweet and pure."

The only problem was that like the many similar products on the market by the late 19th century, it came in jars. To use it, a person dipped his toothbrush into the jar to apply the paste. For a single fella, that worked pretty well; but if he happened to be a family man, well, eewwww!

Fortunately for Washington Sheffield (and for all of us who love our families, but would prefer not to share their dirty mouth germs), the proverbial apple didn't fall far from the tree. Lucius brought the idea of the collapsible paint tube he'd observed in Paris back to his father who soon presented the world with its first tube of toothpaste.

With this major hygiene hurdle overcome, only one question remained, and it plagues humanity to this very day: Do you squeeze the tube from the end or from the middle?

I've been married, very happily, for nearly 14 years now. But like every married couple, we had to learn to live with one another. Of course, that means cobbling together holiday traditions from two separate families and creating something new. It means figuring out how to navigate household responsibilities and how to parent as a team. But it also means coming to a compromise on all those little habits you never even thought about before, like which direction the toilet paper should roll.

Enter the great toothpaste tube war of 2000. When we were first married, my husband and I lived in a drafty brick duplex in Rockford, Illinois. It was a great first home, but it had a tiny bathroom that wouldn't accommodate even an extra tube of toothpaste.

He was raised in a family of meticulous bottom-up tube squeezers. I was raised (apparently by animals) in a home full of willy-nilly toothpaste squeezers. Our tubes were always crumpled any-which-way; and when they approached empty, someone would have to spend time flattening them out to pinch the remaining paste up toward the opening while tightly rolling the end of the tube so the next person wouldn't screw it up again.

Talk about marriage problems. Luckily, my husband married a very generous woman, and we were able to come to a compromise after some (heated) debate. We agreed that the toilet paper would always roll over the top (because that's the way it should be) and that the toothpaste would be squeezed from the end of the tube (because it seemed important to him).

And almost 14 years later, even though our bathroom

storage is now roomy enough to accommodate two tubes of toothpaste, we have stuck with the original deal. I may even admit, in moments of weakness, that it might possibly make a little bit of sense to squeeze the tube his way. But in our current house, we also have the advantage that our children primarily use a different bathroom than we do and also a more bubblegum-ish flavored toothpaste. I admit, it gives me some satisfaction to know that the proverbial apples haven't fallen far from the tree. The boys squeeze their tube of toothpaste willy-nilly from the middle.

The Real Renaissance: Elves, Fairies, and the Golden Age of Piracy

I have long maintained that this is not a serious history blog. Though I do attempt to provide good-*ish* information and have generally completed at least some "research" on the topic, I'm a storyteller first and so I often fill in a few blanks along the way. And, on occasion, I may throw in a few anachronisms that you, intelligent reader, I assume will pick up on.

Still, I think it bears repeating: if you are starting your big school history research project and the first thing you've done is stop by to see what the practical historian has to say about it, you're probably not going to get a very good grade.

That's why I decided recently that I should beef up my credentials a little so that I can provide more reliable, useful information. With that in mind, this past weekend, I attended, for the first time ever, a Renaissance festival. Just for you.

It turns out, I don't live too far from the site of the annual St. Louis Renaissance Faire, a festival that isn't the biggest (that's in Texas where everything is bigger) or best of its kind (or even the top 13 according to the Travel channel), but seemed to me like a good place to start my quest for historical accuracy.

The real Renaissance is that period of time that spans the gap between the Middle Ages and life that is somewhat more recognizable by us modern folk. Generally considered to stretch from the 14th century to the 17th, it started as a cultural explosion in Florence and much like the black plague, spread through all of Europe.

The period is characterized by major shifts in art, science, religion, and education. The people of the Renaissance began to think of the world and of themselves differently. Exactly when and exactly why this shifting began is open to a surprising amount of (kind of hostile, actually) debate among scholars. The whole thing is frankly a little nebulous; so in the interest of making it a little more concrete, here's what I learned when I visited the fair, set in the 16th Century French Village of Petit Lyon:

1. There was an enormous amount of cleavage during the Renaissance. Seriously, it was everywhere, breast tissue spilling over the tops of incredibly tight corsets. I even saw a too-tight corset paired with a pair of sweatpants. So, evidently, there were also no decent tailors.

2. The Renaissance can be marked by the presence of elves, although admittedly this could have been only in France. A lot of elves. Many of them had bows. Some wore jester hats and jingling shoes. Still others had too-tight corsets. But though they varied, they could all be easily identified by their very pointy ears.

3. Bands of singing and dancing Caribbean pirates roamed village streets. They were not the

clandestine thieves you might expect, but rather were garishly dressed, self-identified as pirates, and occasionally performed for royalty.

4. The waffle cone, suggested by many to have been invented in the 1904 World's Fair, was a favorite treat of European royalty during the Renaissance.

5. If one could manage to avoid the elves, there was still the large number of fairies to contend with. So many fairies complete with delicate wings, blue-tinted skin, high-pitched sugary voices, and sparkly magical fairy dust. It was best to avoid these whenever possible.

6. Jousting knights mostly told jokes, especially puns. They *loved* puns. They also enjoyed insulting the attending royalty, who were pretty much cool with it.

7. The most popular food of 16th century France was by far the turkey leg. As most sources claim that the turkey, which is native to the Americas, arrived in Europe in the 17th century, I think we can safely assume that those sources are wrong.

8. King Francois II of France did *not* speak French. I know this because my nine-year-old who only knows a few French phrases had the opportunity to be knighted. When the king addressed him in French, my boy responded politely in the king's own tongue, to which King Francois blushed and quickly changed the subject, in English.

So there you have it, the real Renaissance as best as I can tell. I should caution you, though. If you happen to be starting your big school history project on 16th century France or the Renaissance in general and you start by checking out the St. Louis Renaissance Faire, you're probably not going to get a very good grade. Unless of course you happen to be writing about elves and fairies. In that case, you should be good.

One Really Bad Idea. One Really Good Day

In 1926, in a cozy family kitchen in Faribault, Minnesota, a father by the name of Herbert Sellner entertained his young son Art by sitting him on a chair on top of the kitchen table and then in an example of really bad parental judgment, rocking the table. This is according to Sellner family lore, and yes, Art lived to tell (and probably exaggerate) the tale. And even though to responsible parents everywhere, this sounds like one of the worst ideas possibly ever, the sight of young Art tipping every which way and laughing on top of the table did give Herbert Sellner a *great* idea.

Sellner is the inventor of the Tilt-A-Whirl, which debuted at the 1927 Minnesota State Fair. And even though to nearly anyone with the constitution of a person over the age of 16, the Tilt-A-Whirl sounds like one of the worst ideas possibly ever, it went on to become a feature in carnivals and amusement parks all over the world.

Okay, maybe you don't feel as strongly about the Tilt-A-Whirl as I do, but I would almost rather be sitting in a chair on top of a rocking table than ride on one. But I tell Sellner's story for a couple of reasons. First, it's summertime, which in our house means we do a lot of running back and forth tipping this way and that until we're so dizzy we don't know for sure which way is up, and we feel a little queasy.

I've now survived nearly two weeks of summer break. Don't get me wrong. I love summer. I love baseball and swimming, fireflies and staying up late around a campfire. And yes, I love spending all day playing with my kids.

What I don't love (besides the Tilt-A-Whirl) is the fighting. I mean the "He hit me just because I was bored, so I whacked him in the head first," the "He won't give me a turn on the video game I've just been playing for 45 minutes without a break," and the "He's cheating in the game we just made up that has continuously fluxing rules" kind of fighting.

So in order to spend as little time refereeing the impossible as I can, I keep them busy running every which way until they fall asleep. It was in this spirit that I recently took them to a water park across the river in Illinois that I'd never been to before.

The thing is, you may recall that I developed a stress fracture in my foot a little while back. It's not healing quite like expected, so seven weeks later I'm still wearing a clunky and oh-so-attractive boot, which makes water-parking difficult. I did take it off for a while and floated around the lazy river, thereby entertaining my almost seven-year-old for a good 30 seconds.

Fortunately, one of my teenage nieces graciously agreed to go with us and get tossed around in the wave pool with the boys and ride the great big water slide with my nine-year-old. We all came home that evening sun-drenched and tired, but happy and not fighting. Much.

And this is the second reason I bring up Sellner. Because before he became the inventor of the Tilt-A-Whirl, he was first the inventor of the modern water slide. His Water-Toboggan was a large slide built on a beach and stretched out over water. Riders climbed to the top with a floating sled and then sped down, shooting up to 100 feet across the surface of the water. I don't know about you, but to me that sounds pretty fun.

Sellner's 1923 invention thrilled beach goers everywhere and eventually gave rise to the modern water park. So it's Herbert Sellner I have to thank for one great, mostly conflict-free day of summer. And as long as I keep the boys tipping every which way in this Tilt-A-Whirl season, we should do okay. If I get desperate, I suppose I could always put them in a chair on top of the kitchen table and rock them silly.

Oh, the Places I've Never Gone: A Story of SPAM

I love a good road trip and I confess, I have a little bit of an obsession. I collect brochures. I don't mean that I have a basement full of full-color brochures from every place I've ever visited. That might actually make sense.

I mean that at every hotel, roadside diner, and rest stop, the first thing I do is check out the tourism brochure rack, and I usually pick up at least three or four. Of course I do this in the places where I'm staying for a while, but also in the places I'm just driving through.

And here's the strange part: I almost never go to the places in the brochures. But I love to learn about bizarre little tourist sites that get highlighted on those racks. I guess it's my way of soaking in some of the quirkiness of the communities I am privileged to pass through.

There are the standard places like zoos, waterparks, and outlet malls; and in this part of the country there's usually a cave tour or two. Sometimes those are accompanied by interesting stories. But the ones I like best advertise those truly unique places, the ones that are just weird enough that it's unlikely anyone would ever travel specifically to a particular area just to see them.

My latest find, maybe the best brochure I have ever picked up on a road trip, came from a hotel in Rochester, Minnesota, where we stopped this weekend on our way to watch a community theater musical production that featured one of our very talented nieces.

Obviously, she stole the show, and we were delighted to be there to watch her performance; but I admit, second to that, my favorite part of the trip was the place we didn't go: The SPAM Museum in Austin, Minnesota.

Austin is only about a 45-minute drive from Rochester and not particularly out of the way for a traveler headed back to St. Louis, but it was the last day of our whirlwind weekend road trip. We were anxious to head home. And I was the only one who seemed at all interested in going.

How could I not be? First of all the museum is free; so even if it's not everything it's advertised to be, all you've lost is an hour or so of your time, which you can't ever get back. Still, how can you say no to a tourist destination that boldly proclaims: "Theater! Game Show! Restrooms! IT'S ALL HERE!"

So since my family wouldn't be convinced to tour the museum (okay so it's possible I didn't try *that* hard), I had to research SPAM the old fashioned way and just Google it.

SPAM hit the market in 1937 and soon dominated the canned meat industry. A spiced ham product initially made entirely from pork shoulder, which had been an underutilized cut of meat up to that point in the company Hormel's canned meat products, SPAM received its iconic name from a somewhat suspicious contest.

The winning entry was submitted by an actor named Ken Daigneau who also happened to be the brother of a Hormel Foods vice president. There's no word on whether or not said vice president was in fact the judge of the contest, but Hormel awarded Daigneau $100 for his efforts; and it's a good thing they did because "ham jello" just doesn't sing as well.

Though SPAM (which Hormel claims stands for "spiced ham" and not the "something posing as meat" that some have suggested) took off largely as a wartime food, its real boost into the popular psyche came from Monty Python's famous 1970 SPAM comedy sketch, which period actors with brilliant British accents (I'm sure) reenact daily for a fascinated audience at the SPAM Museum.

Alas, I've never been. Still, I do have the brilliant brochure that both splits into detachable postcards with fun SPAM facts, so you can conveniently invite your friends from all over the world to a SPAM pilgrimage they won't soon forget and also features a helpful map placing the museum into geographical context with the World's Largest Stack of Empty Oil Cans. I haven't managed to collect a brochure advertising that American travel gem yet, but it's definitely on my list of sites to not visit.

August 14, 2014

Absolute Leisure and Peace

In May of 1906, the *Atlantic Monthly* published a piece by American nature essayist John Burroughs who wrote of his experience camping in Yellowstone National Park with President Theodore Roosevelt. The trip itself occurred three years earlier in the spring of 1903; but Burroughs begins his essay by explaining that in the time since, he's not had a moment to sit down and write about it what with all the "stress and strain of [his] life at [home] — administering to the affairs of so many of the wild creatures about [him]."

I can relate to that. I try to post to this blog every Thursday with some new snippet of history and nonsense, but sometimes I don't make it. And now it has been three weeks since my last post. Summer is especially tough because my sons (seven and nine) are out of school; and well, what with the stress and strain of administering to the affairs of the wild creatures about me, I just hadn't gotten around to it until now.

But my family just recently returned from a trip through the western United States, including Yellowstone; and since school started this week, I thought I'd finally take a moment to write about it.

First of all, though my husband had been to the oldest

national park *in the world* several times, the boys and I had never been. Just judging by the variety of license plates we saw and the number of languages we heard, I'm guessing most of you have been. If you haven't, and you ever have the opportunity, you should go.

Because it's weird.

At least that's all most people told me about it before I went. And they weren't wrong. It is weird. It bubbles and boils beneath you and vents its acrid steam and then belches great plumes of water before a crowd that can't help but gasp and cheer, even while realizing that the earth here could actually explode and kill us all.

And then there's the wildlife. Our first night in the park, we camped because we wanted our boys to have that experience. We got our tent all set up and attended an evening ranger program, where we proceeded to learn all the ways bears, elk, and bison can and will kill you. Then we slept in our tent pitched alongside trees that had been marked by bears, elk, and bison. We spent our remaining nights in a lodge.

But Roosevelt and his companions largely didn't. On a brief respite from a westward speaking tour, the president mostly camped in the backcountry. Of course, there were no terribly endangered bison to speak of in the park at that time, and as this was early spring, most of the bears were still hibernating; but there were lots of elk and still a fair number of mountain lions and other predators.

It was the animal life that chiefly interested Roosevelt. According to Burroughs, the president, much to the chagrin of those companions charged with his safety, set off by himself as often as he could to enjoy a quiet picnic lunch alongside a wandering herd. Once while coatless and half lathered in the middle of a shave, Roosevelt rushed to the canyon's edge to watch the treacherous descent of a group of goats headed for a drink from the river below.

Despite the grueling travel over still deep snow in many

parts of the park, the sixteen day detour through Yellowstone apparently left Roosevelt refreshed and more determined than ever to advocate for the nation's natural spaces.

When we were about to leave the park, I admitted to my husband, who had largely planned this trip on his own, that I'd had my doubts about this vacation. It's not that I don't like to animal watch and hike. I do, but I wondered if it would hold the attention of our boys or if we would all be tired and cranky and wishing we'd spent a week at the beach instead.

I was pleasantly surprised. They loved it, almost every minute of it. They delighted in walking past the smelly, gurgling acid pools of a giant super volcano, and they loved craning their necks to spot distant elk herds and bird species they'd never seen or bothered to identify.

We came home refreshed. And I'm delighted to finally take a moment to reflect on the journey. I'm also glad that it didn't take me the three years it took Burroughs, who defended his slow pace by reminding his readers that he didn't have the "absolute leisure and peace of the White House" that allowed Roosevelt to write his own reflections shortly after the trip.

Yep. I bet that's it. If only I were president, I'd have all the time in the world to post.

September 11, 2014

The Sleepless Binge: from Shakespeare to Netflix

On a clear summer night in August of 1863, a young presidential aid named John Hays fought the sleep that threatened to overtake him and accompanied President Abraham Lincoln on a late night stroll through Washington DC. Lincoln was a good strategist, a big picture thinker, and a convicted leader. But he wasn't a very good sleeper.

Throughout his presidency, many nights found him pacing his office or walking through the streets, while the rest of the city slept, sometimes keeping his aids up late with him, regaling them with funny stories or reading to them from his favorite literary works.

This August night, the president led Hays to the Naval Observatory, where the two looked up at the moon and the star Arcturus. Then, we know from the aid's journal, Lincoln next led him back to the Soldier's Home where the Lincolns lived for most of the Civil War and there, began to read to him from Shakespeare's Henry VI and Richard III "until [Hays's] heavy eye-lids caught [Lincoln's] considerable notice, and he sent [Hays] to bed."

Now I like Shakespeare and all; but I value my sleep, so that sounds a little cruel to me. Still I certainly can't blame the president for his insomnia. History suggests that for a time he was treating tummy troubles with mercury-containing pills that would surely have made him edgy and robbed him of a good night's sleep. And he did have a stressful job, during one of the most stressful times in his nation's history.

He couldn't exactly wake up Mrs. Lincoln for company either because (according to a Duke University study conducted not so long ago) women are at much greater risk of heart disease, depression, stroke, and probably just plain crabbiness when they don't get enough sleep.

So this brings me to my last two weeks or so. I haven't been getting enough sleep. I tend to fall asleep okay, but then wake up a few hours later, my mind alive with all kinds of jumbled thoughts about all the things I need to get done, how that's going to be hard to do if I can't get some more sleep, and now (thanks to the folks at Duke University) how I'm going to develop heart disease, depression, and probably have a stroke.

I shouldn't complain. I'm really not affected by insomnia very often, and usually only for a few days when I am; but I always just kind of have to wait it out because it's hard to pinpoint exactly why it strikes. I haven't been ingesting any mercury as far as I know, and I'm not facing any looming deadlines or major life changes. I'm just not sleeping well.

I could lay some of the blame on the appearance of the third season of *Once Upon a Time* on Netflix (because in theory, I could go to bed at a decent hour and not binge watch this guilty pleasure, but of course that's not what I've been doing). I could even attribute my troubles to watching the news as formerly primarily regional problems become increasingly threatening to the stability of the entire world.

And it could just be the dog's fault. He tends to wake up in the middle of the night, too, and stretch and pace for a while, jingling the tags on his collar before settling back into his bed, leaving me wide awake with a million thoughts. Perhaps I should get up and take him for a midnight stroll.

Or maybe I just need to read him more Shakespeare.

Eating America's Homework

My husband tells a story of one of his favorite college professors, a British gentlemen teaching at an American university, who, while assigning a paper, reminded his students that, "English is a borrowed language and [he expected] it to be returned undamaged." The class laughed, and most likely the professor only meant to remind the students that careful editing would be appreciated as he was going to have to read whatever drivel they turned in. But just in case, my husband made sure to incorporate words such as "colour" and "centre" into his work. It was appreciated.

The story is a happy memory because this pseudo-requirement to use the Queen's English was just one funny moment, and perhaps an extra challenge thrown down, in the midst of a really positive classroom experience.

But I suspect Noah Webster, born 256 years ago today, wouldn't have seen it the same way. In 1779, Webster was a young teacher in the early days of a new nation at a time when few children attended school beyond the age of 10 or 11. The schools generally consisted of a single room and served sometimes as many as 70 children with only one teacher. When text books were available, they were British, containing lessons on the geography of England, and even professions of allegiance to King George.

Webster decided to write his own text books, beginning with an age-leveled speller that rejected what he called "the clamour of pedantry" that resulted from the language of the British aristocracy, insisting that American language shouldn't develop from studies of Greek and Latin but rather from the way it is used by the American people.

So with that in mind, after writing a few good old 'Merican text books, Webster decided to tackle a good old 'Merican dictionary. Twenty-two years and 70,000 words later, he had what would eventually transform into one of the most influential English language dictionaries in the world.

Webster's work standardized alternate, more phonetic spellings for many words, making changes such as *colour* to *color* and *centre* to *center*; though, a few attempts at changes like *women* to *wimmin* and *tongue* to *tung* didn't stick, much to the chagrin of American elementary students trying to learn to spell.

Still, Webster's dictionary was fairly well-received. For the first time, an English language dictionary included uniquely American words like *skunk*, *hickory*, and *squash*. And until a national uproar over *Webster's Third International Dictionary's* inclusion of the word *ain't* in 1961, the public pretty much approved of the notion that the American version of the English language should evolve at the direction of the people, just as its government had been designed to do.

Controversy aside, Merriam-Webster dictionaries have long been a staple in American schools and on bookshelves in American homes. I received a copy of the 10th edition of *Merriam-Webster's Collegiate Dictionary* when I graduated from high school, and it has been with me for nearly twenty years, offering me over 215, 000 entries, none of which contains the correct spelling of either *hashtag* or *turducken*.

So perhaps it wasn't such a terrible thing when I walked into my office a couple weeks ago to discover that my dog had pulled the faithful old book off its shelf and commenced to tear it to pieces. The cover is gone, as is a good chunk of the "A" section, including the entry for *ain't*, if it was in the collegiate edition in the first place (alas, I'll never know).

At first I was mad, but as I thought about the history of this reference book, derived as it was from the frustrations of the man some consider to be the father of the American public education system, I realized that my dog ate my homework. Better than that, he ate America's homework.

In celebration of Noah Webster's 256th birthday, I could really use a new dictionary anyway. And I should probably keep it on a higher shelf.

One Step Closer to Rock 'n' Roll

On the West Bank of the Nile at the entrance to the Valley of the Kings, stands the mortuary temple of Hatshepsut, one of only a handful of women who served as Pharaoh in Ancient Egypt. Excavated by Howard Carter in 1903, the temple was designed by architect and all around important advisor Senenmut, who according to historian locker room gossip, may have been Hatshepsut's someone special.

The rumor is far from substantiated; but there's a little evidence that Senenmut might have caused the Pharaoh's heart to flutter, the most overlooked of which, I think, is the fact that near his own tomb, across the river, Senenmut honored his hired musician by having him buried nearby.

The musician's name was Har-Mose, and his coffin can be seen at the Metropolitan Museum of Art. But that's not the most impressive thing found in his tomb because buried with Har-Mose, about 3,500 years ago, was the oldest preserved guitar-like instrument that's ever been found.

The instrument has only three strings, but it has an attached plectrum (or pick) as well as a carved cedar sound box and rawhide soundboard. In other words, it's kind of a guitar. And like most rock stars, Har-Mose must have been pretty attached to his axe since he was buried with it. Or really, his employer Senenmut must have been attached, I'm guessing, because even in Ancient Egypt, a man with a guitar had a good shot at getting the girl, even if she happened to be Pharaoh.

Okay, so that might be a stretch, and I'm pretty sure it wasn't to impress the ladies that at the age of six, our oldest son informed us that he would like to start a rock band. He had it all figured out, he'd explained, providing us with a list of what he would need in order to accomplish his goal. He'd need an electric guitar, of course, as well as a bass guitar. He'd need amplifiers. BIG amplifiers. Naturally, he'd also need a drum set, a keyboard, and a microphone.

We said, "How 'bout let's start with some piano lessons?"

He thought about it for a minute and agreed that could work. And though he's been happily playing piano more or less ever since, he's never really given up his dream of rock 'n' roll. He's already decided he'd like to drum when it comes time to start in the school band, and he's been dropping hints about that electric guitar.

I love music. I studied piano a little when I was young and played the alto sax for about nine years. I'm just not really a guitar person. By that I mean, while I certainly enjoy listening to the guitar, I don't play it or know much about it.

But I love that my son loves music, and I want to encourage his interests when I can; so when he turns ten this week, he is going to totally freak out over his new electric guitar and (not-so-big) amplifier. I have to say, of all the gifts we've ever given him, I'm the most stoked about this one.

I anticipate that as he grows and hopefully becomes a more accomplished musician, adding to his collection the rest of the pieces of his band, and probably a nicer guitar and a MUCH bigger amplifier, this gift will long remain meaningful.

And yes, I realize he will likely use it someday to attract the attention of the ladies. But for now, I'm going to enjoy the fact that I'm the main lady in his life, and I can't wait to hear the first butchered chords and failed attempts as he rocks out.

January 15, 2015

This Ain't My First Rodeo

On July 4, 1888, Juan Leivas showed off his mad cowboy skills to the people of Prescott, Arizona, where the first organized rodeo took place. He performed well, despite the fact that if the great historians of Prescott are to be believed, this was indeed his first rodeo. After the competition, Leivas rode off into the sunset with a silver shield for his efforts to forever be known as the world's first rodeo champion.

But as documented and well-promoted as Prescott's claim to have hosted the first rodeo may be, the good people of Pecos, Texas cry foul. They claim that only a few years after their town's founding, as early as 1883, cowboys gathered during 4th of July celebrations to pit their mad cowboy skills against each other for cash prizes.

Pecos is so serious about its claim that when in 1985 the game *Trivial Pursuit* listed Prescott as the home of the world's first rodeo, the city of Pecos threatened to sue, proving that what is most certainly true is that you should not mess with Texas.

The game stuck with Prescott (so if you ever get that question, you'll know); but to add even more confusion, other rodeo historians (and there are quite a few as it turns out) insist that 16 years before Prescott's rodeo and a year before the founding of the town of Pecos, a group of cowboys from Texas arrived in Cheyenne, Wyoming on July 4, 1872 and put together a friendly competition to unwind and show off some of their mad cowboy skills. And that, of course, was the first rodeo.

Which would be all well and good, except that according to *Field & Farm Journal of Denver*, in 1869, Deer Trail, Colorado hosted an event in which cowboys gathered in an impressive display of mad cowboy skills, competing for a new set of clothes. An Englishman by the name of Emilnie Gardenshire (which is a terrible cowboy name) was said to have taken home the prize at what was surely his very first rodeo.

Then there's a letter, written in 1847 by Captain Mayne Reid from Santa Fe, New Mexico to a friend in Ireland, in which he describes the annual round-up of animals bound for market and calves bound for the branding iron, adding that the cowboys "contest with each other for the best roping and throwing, and there are horse races and whiskey and wine." Sounds like a party to me, and possibly an account of the first rodeo.

I'll leave the arguing to the brave men and women who work within the angry knot of controversy that is the field of rodeo history. I have the feeling those folks have been to the rodeo a time or two.

I have not. In fact, this past weekend, when a rodeo came to a town nearby and my husband bought tickets to take our boys (7 and 10) to their first rodeo, I went to a baby shower instead. I visited with friends I hadn't seen in a while, ate delicious cake, and participated in the sentimental sharing of memories of pregnancies and babies. Not once did I have to smell cow poop, nor did I find myself worried that the shower guests might actually break their necks. I had a good time.

But so did the boys. They returned home that night full of tales of bucking broncos and heroic cowboys. My youngest (who rooted for the animals, even when the necessity of the skills were explained to him) told of feisty calves who made daring escapes from the cowboys attempting to bind their legs. Both boys described in detail the shenanigans of the rodeo clowns, whose silly bathroom humor seemed perfectly geared for the 7 to 10-year-old crowd.

They were so excited it was difficult to get them settled down for the night, and I admit, I was a little sad that I didn't get to experience it with them. No one may know for sure when *the* first rodeo took place; but this was theirs, and it was memorable. I suspect I will not get out of going the next time. I better brush up on my knowledge of mad cowboy skills.

A Sock Full of Mould Juice: How Poor Housekeeping Saves Lives

I have very clear, happy memories of many family vacations throughout my childhood, but there is one not-so-great memory that sticks out in my mind. It was the year my mother decided we needed to first deep-clean the entire house and only then, leave so it would stay that way.

I wasn't a very neat kid. My room was always a disaster with toys and books everywhere and with who knows what growing on the slightly damp, balled up socks in the corner of the closet. As the youngest during that pre-vacation cleaning spree, my job was to scrub window sills and to clean up my disaster of a bedroom. I'm not sure what year it was or what trip we were headed out on, but I do know for certain that we came home to a clean space.

That wasn't the case for Scottish bacteriologist Alexander Fleming when he returned to his lab in September of 1928 after a two-week family vacation. He found the lab exactly as he'd left it, a jumbled mess of half-finished experiments and dirty glassware. It seems Fleming never consulted with my mother on the joys of returning home to a clean space.

After his vacation, Fleming found himself sorting through petri dishes filled with growing *staphylococcus* that had been left in a pile in the corner of the room while he was gone. When he got to one that was overwhelmed by growth of an unidentified mold, he might have simply said, "Ew," and thrown it into the sink, or at least the corner of the closet.

But fortunately, he didn't. Instead Fleming said, "That's funny." As he looked at the dish more closely, he noticed that where the mold thrived, the bacteria didn't. He set to work identifying the funky growth as belonging to the *penicillium* family and hypothesized that the "mould juice" it produced had an antibacterial effect.

In 1929, he changed the name of his antibacterial substance from "mould juice" to the sciencier sounding "penicillin" and published his findings in the *British Journal of Experimental Pathology*. The article went largely unnoticed for several years as Fleming attempted to further his research, only to discover that without some help from a chemist or two, he couldn't be sure that mould juice was worth the effort.

Help arrived shortly after Fleming had officially given up. Pathologist Howard Florey and biochemist Ernst Chain read Fleming's long-overlooked article and began experimenting with Penicillin in mice, finding that it cured them of their mousy bacterial infections. All they needed was a way to mass produce Fleming's mould juice. They headed to America, dropped that pesky "u," and found that Illinois produce was particularly good for growing mold (a point of pride, I've no doubt, for my state of origin).

All three men were awarded a Nobel Prize for the discovery of what remains one of the greatest leaps forward in modern medicine, leading to the discovery and production of many more antibiotics, stopping infections and saving countless lives, all because Alexander Fleming didn't bother to clean his room.

I admit that I have not shared this story with my children.

You see, much to my mother's surprise, I grew up to be a somewhat tidy housekeeper. And my sons definitely complain when I assign them the task of cleaning their disastrous bedrooms (and sometimes the window sills because I have an aversion to the task).

But when my oldest son, who has had a cold for over a week, woke up the other night, screaming with terrible ear pain, I was grateful for the slovenly habits of Dr. Fleming. The next day I took him to the doctor, who looked in his angry ears and prescribed him an antibiotic. He stayed home from school, taking it easy the rest of the day. As he started to feel better, I confess I considered making him clean his room. I didn't because you never know what might be growing on the slightly damp balled up socks in the corner of the closet.

The 2nd Grade Butterfly Effect

First published in *Collier's* magazine in June of 1952, Ray Bradbury's "A Sound of Thunder" went on to become one of the most frequently re-published short science fiction stories of all time, but the concept at its heart was far from new.

The story, set in 2055, centers on a wealthy man who pays to travel back in time in order to hunt a *Tyrannosaurus rex*. The hunt has been well planned. The dinosaur is already destined to die naturally mere moments after the fatal shot, and the safari company has provided platforms designed to elevate the hunt participants off the natural landscape, so their actions in the past may affect as little future change as possible. But despite stern warnings of the dangers of altering the past, the wealthy man loses his cool when faced with T. rex, and in his panic, he leaves the path.

The group returns to the future to discover things aren't quite the same. Words are spelled differently, election outcomes have changed, and humanity's collective outlook is strangely altered. The man then notices in the mud on his boot, a crushed butterfly that apparently died before its time.

Though the concept of tiny alterations in initial conditions affecting significant differences in outcomes (known as chaos theory) was first described by Henri Poincaré in 1890, it was mathematician and meteorologist Edward Lorenz who first applied the term "butterfly effect." He noted that even a very slight change in his data entry (like rounding off a few decimal places) led to drastically different weather model outcomes. It was as if a butterfly flapping its wings caused a miniscule shift in the atmosphere that may eventually lead to the formation of a tornado.

I admit, it sounds a little crazy, and I'm certainly no expert on chaos theory; but I did have the opportunity earlier this week to help chaperone my son's second grade class field trip to the Missouri Botanical Garden's Butterfly House.

Upon arrival, I was handed a clipboard with a checklist of butterfly behaviors we might observe and the names of five second-graders for whom I would be responsible. And that should have been fine. The kids seemed like a good bunch: my son, two other little boys who appeared relatively cooperative, and two sweet, little girls who were all smiles. I was feeling pretty confident about the whole thing.

But then, just as the outer atrium door shut behind us and 25 second-graders along with their teacher, several chaperones, and one butterfly expert loudly sharing important rules (like don't squish the butterflies because it might alter the space-time continuum) were wedged into a tiny butterfly escape-proof airlock, I felt a small hand squeeze my arm.

It was one of the little boys in my group. I'll call him Sam because that's not his name. Sam's eyes were as wide as saucers, his skin pale. "I don't like butterflies," he whispered.

My chaperone training (which consisted of being handed a clipboard) had not prepared me for such a situation. All I could think to do was whisper back, "We'll get through this. I promise."

Right away I could see that Sam didn't believe me, but the butterfly expert had already opened the inner door and the class filed into the steamy atrium. Sam, shaking slightly, fell in line.

He settled into a slow pace, his eyes darting wildly as delicate wings rushed around him. I found myself worrying that as he paced, he would inadvertently squish a butterfly and disrupt the space-time continuum.

While I was busy worrying, an argument broke out between the two girls over who would hold the clipboard. Of course, I told them I would hold onto it, but it was too late. It turns out second-grade girls do not forgive easily.

As I attempted to play referee between them, the second little boy (who evidently had trouble hearing his name above the rush of hundreds of fluttering wings) began to wander aimlessly through the atrium. Determined that the space-time continuum would not be altered on my watch, I did the only thing I could. I carefully ushered the remaining four kids in the direction of the wayward boy.

And that's when my son fell apart. Because the only thing he wanted to do was stand completely still in one place in hopes that a butterfly would choose to land on him, which sadly, it never did.

And so I juggled and chaperoned to the best of my ability for what felt like three hours (though it was really probably about 25 minutes) before we finally escaped the atrium and headed to a classroom, where the butterfly experts mercifully took over.

I'm delighted to report that I walked out of the atrium with all five of my assigned students; and that even though one of them may be scarred for life by the experience, to the best of my knowledge, no butterflies were squished on my watch.

I learned a couple of important things from the experience. First is that second-grade teachers are terribly under-appreciated. And second is that Poincaré, Lorenz, and Bradbury may have been onto something because when a butterfly flaps its wings, whether the space-time continuum is drastically altered or not, one thing is for certain: second grade classes descend into chaos.

This Mermaid's Gotta Swim

On a sunny summer day in 1908, on the crowded Revere Beach in Boston, Massachusetts, Australian swimming sensation Annette Kellerman tangled with the law. As young ladies splashed among the waves with their pretty bathing dresses and bloomers, the 21-year-old Kellerman set out for a swim in a one-piece men's bathing suit that revealed a good portion of her thighs.

Dubbed the "Australian Mermaid," Kellerman was in the midst of an American tour in which she wowed crowds with her diving stunts and with her form-fitting bathing suit (initially with stockings for full leg coverage). When she was arrested in Boston for indecent exposure, she simply explained to the judge that she couldn't "swim wearing more stuff than you hang on a clothes line."

The judge agreed, and Kellerman went on her way toward a career, not just as a Vaudeville performer, but also as a movie actress (including playing the lead in *A Daughter of the Gods*, in which she bared much more than her thighs) and as a health and fitness guru. One Harvard professor (who somehow managed to make a living out of studying the female form, the sly dog) even determined that she was the "perfect woman" because her measurements so closely mirrored the Venus de Milo.

She was a woman way beyond her time, which was after all, a time when women sometimes still used bathing machines (a kind of wheeled dressing room) to enter the water without anyone seeing their voluminous precursors to the itsy-bitsy-teeny-weeny-yellow-polka-dot bikini.

So I suppose womankind owes Ms. Kellerman a debt of gratitude. But as I stole a little time from this busy week of end-of-the-year school programs and projects, so I could do some peaceful shopping for a new swimming suit or two before I start spending pretty much every afternoon at the pool with my kids, I found myself wishing for a little more fabric or maybe some bloomers or even a dressing room on wheels.

There's little that can shake a woman's confidence in her own physical beauty more than looking at herself in a mirror, in bad lighting, wearing little more than her underwear. Still, I'm a swimmer. The sport is one of my great loves, and I am eager every spring to get outside and hit the water, whether I resemble the Venus de Milo or not.

But like Kellerman, I'm pretty practical about my swimwear. I will get out there and brave the racks of the kinds of swimsuits that run the very real risk of falling off in the water and probably ought to get their wearers arrested in Boston for indecent exposure, so I can find a suit that will allow me to move like the American mermaid I was meant to be.

And I think Annette Kellerman would approve. Because even though she was never shy about displaying her own beauty for the world, she was first and foremost a proponent of women's physical fitness. As such, I suspect her attitude toward the teeny-weeny dental floss bikinis available today would be similar to that of her attitude toward the bathing dresses of the early 20th century.

About those she had this to say: "There are two kinds of

bathing suits; those for use in the water and those that are unfit for use except on dry land. If you are going to swim, wear a water bathing suit. But if you are merely going to play on the beach and pose for your camera friends, you may safely wear the dry land variety."

I think I'll stick with the water kind because no one is getting near me with a camera. And this mermaid's gotta swim.

May 28, 2015

Dancing with the Squares

In 1923 America's dance floors were headed for trouble. Ladies were just beginning to wear almost sensible clothing that allowed them to move and swing; jazz was emerging as a fast-paced and exciting music style; and the kids were snuggling close with a good fox trot or waltz and then dancing themselves silly with the Lindy Hop and the Charleston. The morals of a bygone era were fast crumbling away.

One man decided he was going to do something about it. The father of the auto industry and master of the assembly line, Henry Ford, figured if he could put together a car one piece at a time, then he could put wholesome American culture back together the same way, one dance step at a time. And so he set out on a crusade to bring back the good old-fashioned square dance.

American square dance has a muddy history, but it generally traces its roots back to the coordinated group dances of England in the early 1600s. Of course when settlers brought it with them to the new world, it took on a uniquely American flavor. A caller announced the moves, which were given French names (because that seemed likely to irritate the English), like "promenade," "allemande," and "dos-à-dos" (which quickly became "do-si-do" because that seemed likely to irritate the French).

As America became more urbanized, square dancing faded, but Ford saw the dance as a way to promote exercise as well as genteel manners. He hired a square dance caller by the name of Benjamin Lovett to teach square dance full time in Dearborn, Michigan and required his employees to engage in the activity. He also sponsored square dance programs in many public schools, on college campuses, and over the radio waves.

It worked. The dance started to catch on. Soon ladies and gentlemen were lined up in groups on the dance floor to bow to their partners and perform coordinated dance steps with very little touching and plenty of room for the Holy Spirit. The dance's popularity continued through World War II and the following decade before it began once again to fade. But I think it's going to surge again, led by an army of enthusiastic Missouri fourth graders.

My kids are officially out of school for the summer now, but these last few weeks leading up to the last day have been busy.

There've been awards ceremonies and book fairs and pizza parties and field days. And yes, square dancing.

Last week, my fourth grader (now officially a fifth grader!) participated in Missouri Day at school. I don't know if this is a state required thing or if it's just something our school does, but the kids were taken through a series of activities to help them learn about all things Missouri. Because I am a dedicated parent (or a sucker who can't say no), I volunteered to help.

It turns out the official state folk dance of Missouri is the square dance (as opposed to other kinds of American folk dances . . . go on, try to name one). In fact, 24 states have declared the square dance their state folk dance, and it would be 25 if Minnesota would just bite the bullet and make it official since it was proposed in both 1992 and 1994, but I suppose something this important shouldn't be rushed.

So I went to the school to help the fourth graders learn to

square dance. Of course, I don't believe I've ever square danced. I went to fourth grade in the state of Illinois (where the square dance is also the state folk dance), and no one seemed to care whether or not I learned this critical life skill.

Basically, my job was to try to help two groups of eight kids interpret the instruction given by the elderly square dance caller. Allegedly.

What I *really* did was attempt to convince a bunch of ten-year-olds that they probably won't die from touching the hands of another ten-year-old of the opposite sex, and failing that, how they might effectively swing their partner without actually coming into contact with him or her.

And I think once they figured it out, the kids had a pretty good time. Henry Ford would have been proud.

June 11, 2015

The Stuff of Family Vacation Legend

By 1903, Henry Lee Higginson, most well known for founding the Boston Symphony Orchestra, had grown sick and tired of crazy drivers, in their newfangled automobiles, flying down the streets near his summer home, completely ignoring the posted speed limit of 15 miles per hour.

Never shy about contacting his representatives in government to register a complaint or share unsolicited advice, Higginson submitted a petition entitled, "A Petition Relative to Licensing Automobiles and Those Operating the Same." The way he saw it, there was no way to hold those dadgum irresponsible drivers accountable unless there was a reliable way to identify them.

His suggestion was that all automobiles should be required to be registered with an accompanying fee of two dollars each year. Higginson's very concern was already being discussed by Massachusetts lawmakers, particularly by the newly formed Automobile Department, which included Higginson's nephew Fredrick Tudor.

Apparently, if you're a concerned citizen (or a grumpy old man), it's good to be a connected one because that same year, the first state-issued license plate in the entire United States was issued, a steel plate coated in porcelain with a cobalt blue background and raised white number. Across the top were the words, "MASS. AUTOMOBILE REGISTER," because even the people who live there can't spell Massachusetts.

Massachusetts wasn't the first state to require license plates. New York had been using them for a couple years already, but only required that drivers make an identification tag themselves, which meant that everyone just ended up with the same vanity plate: "BY OFFCER."

So when Fredrick Tudor rolled off the lot with his brand new state issued-license plate, reading "1," it was kind of a big deal. Other states, including New York, borrowed the idea, and soon it was nearly impossible for dadgum crazy drivers to rip through Henry Higginson's neighborhood at 16 miles per hour with impunity.

At last, the state could make a few bucks by issuing plates that said "C U L8R" and could more easily identify vehicles that needed to be identified. But we all know the real reason we have state-issued license plates on our vehicles is because families heading out in the old Subaru for summer fun and togetherness need some way to pass the time. They need the license plate game.

It's not much of a game, really, just writing down every state represented on the road through the seemingly endless hours of travel. But let me tell you, the excitement when everyone spots Alaska in the middle of Georgia is the stuff of family vacation legend.

My family and I recently took just such a trip. A couple days after the kids got out of school, we took off on the 14 or so hour drive for Universal Studios in Florida. It was a fantastic vacation, full of movie magic and all things Harry Potter, a great way to kick off the summer. And we saw a fair number of plates along the way, an awesome 44 out of 50 states, along with a good portion of Canadian provinces.

When we drove out west last summer to Yellowstone, we saw all but one state (apparently the good people of Delaware don't get out much); but I still think we did fairly well. On our Florida drive, we didn't see Vermont, New Hampshire, Nevada, South Dakota, or Utah. If you're from any of those states, you're missing a great trip. We also failed to find Hawaii, but I suppose that would be a tough drive (even tougher than Yellowstone, apparently).

We saw plenty of Massachusetts on this trip, but not plate #1. It is still an active registration, held by a relative of Fredrick Tudor, and I suppose Henry Lee Higginson, too. Whoever has it now, I sure hope he obeys posted speed limits.

June 25, 2015

No Practical Application Whatsoever

I suspect my windshield wipers are possessed. Last week was an extremely wet week here in the Midwestern US. It was the kind of week when baseball fans wait through rain delays, swimming pools sit unused, and drivers are constantly frustrated that the ever-present swish-swish of wiper blades never quite syncs with the beat of the song on the radio.

So on Thursday I made the awful decision to cancel a trip to Grant's Farm to feed the baby goats. My youngest son had been looking forward to the visit all week. His big brother was spending a very wet week at camp, and this was a special trip for just the two of us. He was heartbroken, and I felt terrible; but of course, there was nothing I could do because sometimes the weather wins.

Fortunately, that wasn't the attitude of can-doer Mary Anderson of Birmingham, Alabama, when she visited New York in the early 1900s. It was a terribly snowy and icy day when she set out to see the city sights, grateful, I suspect, to be in the relative comfort of a street car. That is until the driver slid aside the iced-over windshield to get a better view of where he was going, and she received a blast of icy wind in the face.

Real estate developer, cattle rancher, winemaker, and all around spunky lady, Anderson thought there had to be a better way to deal with the visibility issue. Right there on the streetcar, she began to sketch some ideas.

After a number of tries, she finally came up with a prototype that worked; and on November 10, 1903, Mary Anderson was awarded a US patent for her "window cleaning device for electric cars and other vehicles to remove snow, ice, or sleet from the window."

What she had devised was a set of wood and rubber wiper arms the driver could drag across the windshield to clear it of debris with just the pull of a lever. Unfortunately for Ms. Anderson, the automobile wouldn't really catch on in the US for another ten years or so. None of the manufacturers she approached was interested in her idea, citing concerns the device would be a dangerous distraction to the driver if the swish-swish didn't sync up with the beat on the radio. One Canadian company even informed her that the invention had no practical application, a proclamation for which I have to assume someone eventually got fired.

Though Mary Anderson's patent expired before she could make any money from her window cleaning device, she is usually credited as the first inventor of the windshield wiper. She was followed by a number of other inventors with a number of other patents. And obviously, wipers did eventually catch on, becoming fairly standard automobile accessories by 1919, proving remarkably practical and applicable.

Except for when they become possessed. This past Saturday, the clouds finally parted, and we took advantage of the sunny day to go to Grant's Farm and feed the baby goats, this time as a whole family. It was a great day, but I guess the windshield wipers on my car disagreed because on the way home, they turned on by themselves; and despite my best efforts, they've not stopped since.

Though I like to think I am a pretty spunky lady, I am not

as mechanically minded as Mary Anderson was. Still, I am willing to accept there may be an explanation that is more mechanical than spiritual for the behavior of my windshield wipers. My husband has thankfully formulated a few ideas of how to fix them when he gets the chance. I hope it's sometime soon because for now, I am that eccentric lady who is driving through the sunshine with my wipers on low intermittent. I find they're terribly distracting. Their swish-swish never syncs up to the beat on the radio, and they have no practical application whatsoever.

The Mischievous Use of Pyrotechnics

Early this week, the signs began popping up in my town. I noticed them first at the busiest intersections, but soon they spread to public buildings, the entrances to subdivisions, and even as a postcard in our mailboxes. This Independence Day, my town is going to try something new.

The sale and use of fireworks is legal in the state of Missouri, but each town has its own ordinance regarding them. In fact, many municipalities ban them altogether, which doesn't seem like such a bad idea when you consider that fireworks are responsible for an average 10,000 injuries in the US every July and cause somewhere in the neighborhood of $32 million in property damage.

But I guess danger is part of the attraction. At least one story about the not-entirely-clear origin of fireworks tells us that between 600 and 900 AD, Chinese alchemists, who were already adept at blowing stuff up, were trying to develop the elixir of life by heating various combinations of sulfurous mixtures and instead, managed to scorch their hands and faces and burn down their laboratory. The alchemists made note of the combination that had caused such an incident, warning it should never ever be mixed again.

Then, because guys like to blow stuff up, they proceeded to experiment with it anyway until they figured out that if the dangerous mixture were placed in a tube, open on one end, they could produce pretty sparks that made them say "ooh" and "ah."

Despite the best "don't try this at home" warning the Chinese alchemists could muster, fireworks spread through the world and the centuries, getting fancier and fancier along the way, until Captain John Smith of Jamestown fame allegedly set off a display in 1608, and fireworks had officially arrived on the shores of North America.

That was all fine until the early 1700s, when the citizens of Rhode Island took it too far. Evidently Rhode Islanders of the day found it hilarious to load up on explosives at the local fireworks tent and pull off all kinds of explosive shenanigans. The more well-mannered citizens of the colony were not amused; and in 1731, officials issued the first ordinance in the would-be US, banning the "mischievous use of pyrotechnics."

I wasn't in Rhode Island in 1731, so I don't know how the ordinance was received or enforced; but I suspect there were those who went ahead and blew stuff up anyway, probably in the middle of the night, when the well-mannered people were sound asleep, at least until their neurotic dogs snapped to attention and went bananas over the noise.

That's what our new and improved city ordinance is supposed to address. Because ever since 1776, when John Adams said it should be, the 4th of July has always been a fireworks kind of holiday in the US. And guys still like to blow stuff up. So what our town has decided is that even though it is illegal to use or even possess fireworks within the town limits, that restriction will be lifted for a few hours on the 4th.

At exactly 5 pm, guys who like to blow stuff up can cross the city line with their trucks filled from their runs a couple miles up the highway to the fireworks tent and scorch their own hands and faces to their hearts' content.

Not being a guy who likes to blow stuff up, I admit I don't really get the obsession, but I suppose the ordinance is fair. It gives folks the opportunity to celebrate, hopefully encourages them to practice caution as they should, and demonstrates respectful consideration of those who may have difficulty coping with stuff blowing up around them.

And after our window of allowable fireworks frivolity closes at 10 pm, law enforcement will be out in droves to lay the smack down on anyone mischievously using pyrotechnics. By then, my neurotic dog and I will hopefully be sound asleep.

July 16, 2015

Smarty Pants and the Bird Brained Scheme

My youngest son is fixing to turn eight soon. I think I have mostly come to terms with this, balancing that inevitable feeling of loss a mother experiences when her children begin to rely on her less with the joy and pride of watching it happen.

And he has so far stuck a little closer to me than his older brother, whom if he had his choice this summer, might be away at a different camp every week and involved in every activity he can think of.

Because my eldest is so keen to branch out, my younger son and I have gotten to spend a lot of one-on-one time so far this summer. It's been fun, mostly. Like all children, he has his exasperating moments; but he really is a great kid, smart, thoughtful, and delightfully funny.

A week or so ago we dropped big brother at day camp and headed for the zoo. My youngest is fascinated by animals. He'll watch them for hours, making note of their behaviors and asking really smart questions, so this was the perfect day trip for the two of us.

But as we made our way back to the new polar bear exhibit, my son was more interested in birds. I'm not talking about the zoo birds with clipped wings and identification bracelets. His attention was captured by the plain old Missouri birds that fly freely in and out, visiting the concession stands, so they can eat the fallen French fries.

He walked along happily identifying all the little birds that crossed our path, and like any good mother, I feigned interest. That is until we saw a European starling. When he saw that one, he huffed, "Stupid starling. That's all Shakespeare's fault."

And that's when I realized, I must have really been listening. I stopped walking. Because if your very nearly eight-year-old child references Shakespeare, you pay attention, right?

So I asked, "What's Shakespeare's fault?"

"The American invasion of the European Starling," he replied, as though I were incredibly stupid for asking the question.

Now you have to understand, I hold degrees in both zoology and literature. As far as I know, my almost-eight-year-old holds degrees in neither, so he might have been right. I might have been incredibly stupid to ask the question, but I had to know what he was talking about. I asked him to elaborate. This, along with a few details I filled in later, is the story he told me:

In March of 1890, German immigrant, pharmaceutical manufacturer, Shakespeare lover, and bird enthusiast Eugene Schieffelin released 60 imported starlings into New York's Central Park. Schieffelin was a member of The American Acclimatization Society, a group dedicated to introducing the charming birds of Europe into America, so it would feel more like home.

As one of the many species of birds mentioned by Shakespeare (in Act 1, scene 3 of *Henry IV, Part 1* in case you want to look it up), the starling made the list; and though none of the previous bird introductions had been successful, the starling was made of tougher stuff.

What started out as a population of 60 has become a population of over 200 million invasive, shiny-headed, avian invaders, the nemesis of blue birds and woodpeckers, of farmers and airline pilots. They've even been known to out-compete the redwing blackbird for fallen French fries at the zoo concession stand.

I asked my son how he knew this story. He rolled his eyes and explained that he'd read it in at least two different books. And that's how I learned the history of the American invasion of the European Starling, and also why it is you shouldn't let your smarty pants kids read.

Because that seven-year-old will soon be eight, and his pants are only going to get smarter.

August 20, 2015

Six Hundred Feet of Hyperbole

In the winter of 1678, Father Louis Hennepin became the first white man to view Niagara Falls in person. He'd probably read descriptions written by others, recounting Native American tales that were supported by the distant roar of a great deal of crashing water; but he was the first European to describe first-hand what he saw.

And it must have been a pretty awe-inspiring sight. He begins, "Betwixt the Lake Ontario and Erie, there is a vast and prodigious cadence of water, which falls down after a surprising and astonishing manner, insomuch that the Universe does not afford its parallel."

Father Hennepin goes on to describe how wild beasts, getting caught up in the current, are cast over the edge to fall 600 feet without so much as a barrel for protection.

A few months later, Henry de Tonty visited Niagara Falls and estimated its height at about five hundred feet. And ten years after that, Baron Louis Armand de Lom D'Arce Lahontan said of the Falls, "'Tis seven or eight hundred foot high..."

Of course, all of these early explorers were wrong. By a lot. Horseshoe Falls is actually an average of only 188 feet tall (still a long way for an unfortunate beast or a crazy person in a barrel to tumble), which means it doesn't even crack the top 500 of tallest waterfalls on Earth, let alone in the entire universe.

But I understand the exaggerated estimates of some of the early accounts. My husband and I recently left the kids with grandparents and traveled to the world's first honeymoon capital to celebrate our 15th wedding anniversary. I saw the Falls once when I was a teenager, but this was his first trip. We stayed on the (prettier) Canadian side, a couple miles down river from the Falls and followed a very nice paved walkway toward them. As the roar of rushing water grew, he squeezed my hand more tightly; and when he caught his first glimpse of American Falls (a mere 70 to 100 feet high), he simply said, "Wow!"

Then we rounded the bend toward Horseshoe Falls, and he was momentarily out of any words at all (I guess he doesn't have quite the way with words that Father Hennepin did and never thought to describe the plight of wild beasts plummeting to their deaths). But then maybe the right words to describe that kind of sheer natural power don't exist outside of hyperbole.

Like later explorers to the area, my husband (who is also not as spatially challenged as Father Hennepin) probably could have made a fairly reasonable guess at the height, partially because his travel companion had already picked up a dozen or so brochures about the area. And like us, later arrivals either grabbed a brochure at the welcome center or didn't manage to see any wild beasts tumble over the edge, so their estimates wound up closer to the truth. In 1750, Swedish botanist Petre Kalm, in a letter to a friend in Philadelphia, belittles Father Hennepin, calling him "the Great Liar" and going on to report the (closer) height of 137 feet.

But personally, I think Father Hennepin had it right, because regardless of what taller waterfalls may exist in the world, or may yet be discovered in the wider universe, as far as this spatially challenged writer is concerned, Niagara is vast and prodigious, surprising and astonishing, unparalleled in the Universe, and is at least 600 feet tall.

Fire Hydrants, Creepy Inventors, and Sharknadoes: Why You Should Travel with a Writer

Last week, I wrote about the wonderful anniversary trip my husband and I took to the impossibly beautiful and powerful Niagara Falls. And it really was a great trip, complete with a bicycle wine tour through the Niagara wine region and all the romance you might expect from the first honeymoon capital of the world.

But the trip didn't end there. Because if you happen to marry a historical fiction writer (which you'd only do if you have a quirky sense of adventure), then you occasionally have to make a side research trip.

Fortunately, my husband does have a quirky sense of adventure and is generally up for the occasional odd research side trip. So after the falls, we headed next to the little town of Lockport, New York to take a ride down the Erie Canal.

That's where I was introduced to Birdsill Holly. In 1863, in the then booming canal town, hydraulic engineer and inventor extraordinaire Birdsill Holly brought together several of his previous inventions and introduced the world to his Fire Protection and Water System.

Holly wasn't the first person to patent a fire hydrant. That honor probably goes to an engineer by the name of Frederick Graff, Sr., who allegedly patented a hydrant design in 1801, though history may never know for certain because the record of it was destroyed (ironically) by a patent office fire.

What Holly can be credited with, however, is putting together a system of pumps powered by water turbines and steam engines to bring high pressure water to hydrants placed throughout a town. He started in Lockport, but several cities liked what they saw, and Holly's system was soon in place in major cities across the nation eventually including Chicago, which unfortunately rejected the system until after the great fire of 1871 when it quickly came around to the idea.

Now I don't know about you, but despite the fact that Holly is largely responsible for the introduction of modern fire protection and steam-powered central heating systems, and was a friend of and occasional collaborator with Thomas Edison, I'd never heard of him.

And it turns out the reason why may be because nobody (except perhaps Edison who was impressed by the man's genius) seemed to like him very much. Holly made himself a social outcast shortly after setting up his company in Lockport by divorcing his wife and marrying his ward Sophia who was around 12 at the time. Even by Woody Allen standards, that's pretty creepy.

And then there was the free whiskey he provided for the low-wage workers who dug out the large tunnel through which he supplied hydromechanical power to three Lockport businesses including the Holly Manufacturing Company. His logic was that he could not be held accountable for accidents if his workers chose to be drunk on the job.

But at least he limited how much whiskey was given to the "powder monkeys" (young boys employed to pack and ignite explosives in hard to reach areas because they were 1.smaller 2. faster and 3. more expendable). He only allowed the children half the whiskey that the adult workers were encouraged to consume every hour.

Of course, it turned out that industrial hydromechanical power was short-lived, as easier energy-producing methods came along soon after; but the tunnel (made sort of famous because it's featured in *Sharknado 2: The Second One*, which I haven't seen and now fear I'll have to watch sometime) is still open for tours.

After our thoroughly informative ride down the Erie Canal, we toured the man-made Lockport Cave and learned all about the man who had it constructed, including the wonderful piece of information that the Holly Manufacturing Company, producer of fire hydrants and provider of fire protection systems throughout the nation, eventually burned to the ground. And the citizens of Lockport thought that was pretty funny.

In just a quick (and frankly not exactly exhaustive) Internet search, I have not been able to find reference to that part of the story, but I did with my own eyes see the remains of the destroyed building's foundation and a picture of the blaze.

And that, my friends, is why you should consider traveling with a historical fiction writer. Because you never know what characters you may meet and what great little stories you might discover when you set out on a quirky little research side trip.

September 24, 2015

Pickled History Scraped from the Bottom of the Barrel

On October 21, 1805, the British Royal Navy, under the leadership of Admiral Horatio Nelson, achieved what has been often identified as its most decisive naval victory of the Napoleonic Wars at the Battle of Trafalgar. But the victory came at a price because Admiral Nelson had been shot by a French marksman and soon died with the words, "Thank God, I have done my duty," on his lips.

Like most important men of the era, who had the misfortune to die at sea, the admiral was placed in a barrel of brandy for safekeeping on the trip home aboard his ship, *Victory*. Then the HMS *Pickle*, a schooner that had been present during the battle, was sent ahead to deliver the news that the navy had been victorious and that the admiral had been, well, pickled.

King George III was delighted with the news of the victory, but was purportedly sad to have lost Admiral Nelson, a hero whose memory lives on in the country for which he so nobly fought and died and that is still dotted with tributes to his heroism.

Perhaps the most bizarre tribute to the memory of the admiral is not a monument, however, but instead comes in the form of a tale that evolved from his final voyage, the one he took soaking in a barrel of brandy.

By the late 19th century, a strange saying had emerged from the Royal Navy. If one were caught sneaking an illicit drink, he would be said to have been "tapping the admiral." I can almost hear you saying, "Oh, that's where that comes from." And now I can almost see the disgusted face you're making as you realize what the rest of that story must entail.

Apparently, sailors flush with victory, and probably mourning the loss of friends as well, like to get their drink on. Never having served in the navy myself, I will just have to take the tale-tellers' words for it. As the story goes, these sailors *really* needed to get their drink on, and they weren't about to let good brandy go to waste over one dead admiral.

As the ship sailed, the crew took turns siphoning off bits of the brandy; so much so that when the admiral finally arrived home and the barrel was opened, he was still perfectly preserved, but there wasn't a drop of brandy left.

First of all, gross. Second of all, I think it's pretty safe to assume it never really happened. Again, I've never served in the navy, but I'm acquainted with several people who have, and what I do know is that most of them like to tell tales.

Though various versions of this story are splashed across the Internet, I first encountered it a while ago in a book I was reading as part of my research for the novel I'm currently writing. And then very recently, as I was reading through another (quite different) source for the same project, I stumbled on it again.

I find that one danger of writing historical fiction is that often the story I want to write gets hijacked by my research, by the stories I find along the way (sometimes again and again) that really want to be shared, but that have no place in the book I'm working on. I'm sorry to disappoint any of you out there who might one day read my book, but Admiral Nelson and his barrel of brandy are not in it.

The story behind "tapping the admiral" is fascinating not because it's true (again, gross), but because someone was devilish enough to make it up in the first place. And I would hate to think, dear reader, that you might someday find yourself at a party, sipping a drink (perhaps even brandy) without this story handy to pull out and share.

So here it is, one of the little legends drifting around in the great barrel that contains the tale I'd rather tell. Someday, after I've reached the end of the long, winding road toward a final published work, I hope you'll enjoy the pickled remains. In the meantime, I will occasionally have to siphon off a little of the excess because unlike the sailors who tell them, good stories should never be wasted.

October 1, 2015

A Hyena Caught in a Gin Trap

On November 6, 1745, Scotsman James Reid, who had been found guilty of treason and inciting a riot, was hanged in York. Reid had been a participant in the Jacobite Uprising that sought to restore the Stuart dynasty (and Catholicism) to the British throne, an uprising that finally failed at the Battle of Culloden in the Highlands of Scotland.

Nearly 600 men were captured and taken back to England to face prosecution. But Reid's case stands out because his defense was that he carried neither gun nor sword on the battlefield. He was guilty of nothing more, he claimed, than playing the bagpipes. The court debated; but in the end, it ruled that since Highlanders never marched without a piper to lead the charge, the bagpipe was a weapon of war.

It may not seem that strange to view the instrument that way, as the reaction to bagpipes can often seem similar to the debate over the control of firearms.

Over the years there have been a number of attempts to restrict the playing of bagpipes, from Englishman Clive Hibberts' ultimately unsuccessful 1999 "Campaign Against Bagpipes" to the city of Edinburgh's 2008 threat to arrest anyone playing the pipes on the Royal Mile, a move that eventually led to street musicians being forced to sign acceptable behavior contracts with the city. In parts of Edinburgh, officials have gone so far as to prohibit the playing of even recorded bagpipe music through outdoor speakers of businesses.

And in New Zealand in 2011, bagpipes were added to the list of banned items (a list that includes flares and air horns) at the Rugby World Cup. Because even though bagpipes are part of a long, noble tradition, beloved by perhaps dozens of people, a lot of us might agree with sportscaster Miles Davis who compared the sound of the bagpipes to "a hyena caught in a gin trap."

While I don't mind the occasional bagpipes in an outdoor ceremonial setting (that I can pretty quickly excuse myself from), I tend to fall into the hyena camp. So imagine my excitement when my eight-year-old informed me he would very much like to learn to play this most delightful of Scottish instruments.

It didn't come as a total surprise. His iPod is filled with bagpipe music, and it's not uncommon to find him rocking out to "Scotland the Brave." He's even suggested before that he might want to learn. He's just never sounded this serious. So I did what any loving, supportive parent would do.

I told him he would have to wear a skirt.

He wasn't dissuaded.

I told him the skirt would have to be a purple plaid because according to his grandfather, that is the family tartan.

He was still pretty adamant.

I told him he couldn't wear underwear under his purple plaid skirt.

He grinned.

I don't dare tell him that his favorite instrument has been declared in a court of law to be a weapon of war because this is a battle I fear I will lose. It turns out, he's got a lot of people on his side. I've had offers to borrow a chanter, so he can begin to learn before we invest in the full instrument. I've had friends send me links to college scholarship opportunities for bagpipe players. He's even received multiple invitations from family and friends to practice at their homes, invitations he will be accepting. Often.

Because I'm a loving, supportive mom and I truly believe, or at least I sincerely hope, if he tries it out, he will lose interest. If he doesn't, I guess I'll get him a purple kilt, make him sign an acceptable behavior contract, and learn to love the sound of a hyena caught in a gin trap.

October 22, 2015

Half Ghost, Half Scarecrow, But All Witch: A Case of the Heebie Jeebies

In 1968, *Washington Evening Star* editor Philip Love and his wife attempted to uncover a large piece of evidence in a very old mystery. What they were looking for was an 875-pound rock located somewhere in the woods to the south of Leonardtown, Maryland, that was said to hold the form of the hand of a murdered witch who had cursed the town more than 270 years before.

According to legend, the impression belonged to a woman named Moll Dyer, who traded healing herbs and lived on the outskirts of Leonardtown, largely depending on the generosity of its citizens for her survival. In part because she was unattractive and in part because she gave everyone the heebie jeebies, it was generally believed she was a witch.

The accusation wasn't uncommon in the era, particularly in Maryland, which had tried a number of women for witchcraft and had even executed one. But what was uncommon about 1696, the year Moll Dyer allegedly squished her handprint into a solid rock, was the extremely harsh winter the people of Maryland experienced.

As the dim cold days and long snowy nights dragged on, suspicion began to grow in the town that their devastating weather pattern had been summoned by the witch in their midst, the woman who was said to fly above the town at night, "half ghost, half scarecrow, but all witch," casting her nefarious spells on the local children.

By February of that year, when the snow came down hard and fast yet again, producing rare and heebie-jeebie-inducing snowstorm thunder, the non-witch citizenry of Leonardtown had had enough. They grabbed their torches and their pitchforks, and they burned Moll Dyer's house to the ground, driving her into the bitter cold with nothing but the clothing on her back.

Her body was found a few days later, frozen solid, one hand outstretched, the other pressed into the boulder where she fell, cursing her tormentors.

Now I can't say whether there's any truth to the tale of poor Moll Dyer, and I hope there's not. There isn't great evidence that anyone by that name existed in the area, though there were some Dyers, and records from that period are often a little sketchy. The tale was handed down orally for 160 years before a written record of the name turns up in a deed identifying a portion of land as "Moll Dyer's Run."

But to some extent, most of the residents of the area seem to believe it. Or at least they're a little nervous about tromping through the woods south of town where bizarre weather events, unexplained accidents, and heebie-jeebies abound. Some insist that on particularly cold nights, you can even see Moll Dyer walking through her woods in a particularly unfriendly mood.

Personally, I'm kind of a skeptic about these types of stories; but my husband, who has spent most of his life in the

Midwest, did spend several formative early elementary years in southern Maryland. While putting this story together, I casually asked him if he'd ever heard of the Leonardtown witch. His eyes got big and he asked, "Do you know where I grew up?"

I'm a little directionally challenged anyway; and though I've heard him mention the road he lived on and the name of his school, I had to admit I didn't know what town or precisely where in the state it was located. So he explained to me that he lived on the outskirts of Leonardtown, Maryland, just to the south, across the street from a wood he was warned never to enter and where he'd always believed strange things happened.

And that's when I got the heebie jeebies.

But thanks to the efforts of Philip Love, you don't even have to venture into the forbidden wood to experience the tale of the unfortunate witch yourself because he did finally locate the stone on which Moll Dyer was said to utter her final curse. Since 1972, it has been sitting, without much pomp, in front of the courthouse in downtown Leonardtown.

Rumor has it that if you squint really hard and look at it from just the right angle, you can convince yourself there's a handprint visible in the stone. And if you're the sort of person who might do this kind of thing, you can even place your own hand in the outline. Just know the experience will probably leave you with a good case of the heebie-jeebies.

November 5, 2015

Straight Up Infestation: A Motivational Tale

I don't know about you, but I'm glad it's finally November, a time for cooking up a big pot of soup, building a fire in the fireplace, and reflecting on the many blessings for which we are thankful. Oh, and also for cleaning.

It seems to me that if there is an autumn equivalent to spring cleaning, it happens in the early part of November. Before the cold really sets in and the rush of holiday hosting and merry-making kicks off, it feels like the right time to de-clutter and scrub and organize, a time to chase away the Halloween gloom and the millions of stupid, little plastic spider rings your kids brought home from classroom parties, trunk-or-treats, and fall festivals.

And I'm talking about A LOT of stupid, little plastic spider rings here. I don't know precisely how many came crawling into my house during the last days of October this year, but I have to assume it was a fair few (thousand) because every time I've been cleaning up a storm and I think I about have it done, I find more.

They ambush me from the dark recesses of my kitchen cabinets, scuttle into the corners of rooms I could swear I've already mopped, and creep out of the couch cushions when I finally sit down to relax.

To be clear, I don't have a particular phobia of spiders. I am not the kind of woman who runs screaming from a room at the sight of one, begging the nearest man to kill it for me. In fact, as long as they aren't too big (because let's face it, eight legged critters are not aesthetically pleasing—I'm looking at you, Mr. Giant Squid!), I'm usually content to leave them well-enough alone, knowing that they are anxious to eat other little critters I'd rather not live with.

It turns out spiders may be good for more than just mosquito-eating, too, because in 1306 (or 1313 according to some versions), Robert the Bruce, the king who famously led the Scots in their first war for independence from England, found himself in a pretty miserable place.

His campaign for independence wasn't going well. He'd been defeated in battle five times in a row and was hiding in a cave, considering whether it was all worth it. That's when he spied a small spider working to spin a web across a wide gap. Robert watched the critter fail to jump the gap five times; but on the sixth time, she (because heroic spiders are named Charlotte) successfully made the jump.

Motivated by the spider's determination and eventual success, Robert the Bruce dusted himself off and tried again, leading a far outnumbered Scottish force to victory against the English at the Battle of Bannockburn and eventually to the recognition of Scottish independence.

A version of the story first turns up in the 1643 *History of the House of Douglas*, in which the entire experience of the spider is assigned to Sir James Douglas, an ally and close friend to Robert (like the kind of close friend that carries your embalmed heart into battle after you die, but that's another story). Robert was apparently inserted into the tale in 1827 by Sir Walter Scott.

But the story is well-known by English and Scottish school children, in the same way that American children know of young George Washington's refusal to lie about chopping down a fictional cherry tree. And whether it's true or not, the tale teaches the valuable lesson that success often requires perseverance.

At least that's what I'm going to choose to take from it. Because no matter how many stupid plastic spider rings I have to dig out of my couch cushions and surreptitiously throw away while my children aren't looking, I will get my house cleaned up in time for the holidays. Maybe not on the first attempt or on the second, third, fourth, or fifth, but I'm sure my perseverance will pay off in the end.

December 3, 2015

Controversial Christmas Merry-Making

It's that time of year once again. The giant balloons have bobbed down 6th Avenue, leading Santa to Macy's on 34th. The door buster Black Friday deals (many of which now start on Thanksgiving Thursday) have largely expired. Even the last of the leftover turkey and pumpkin pie has finally been consumed.

Now the lighted Christmas geese have landed in the front yard. A large artificial evergreen resides in my living room, topped with a blinking star and candy cane. As I look around at my glittery surroundings, I'm filled with nostalgia and anticipation.

And also panic. As much as I have accomplished in the past week to prepare for the coming holiday, I'm also staring down a long list of to-dos. In the coming weeks, I'll be baking and hosting and shopping and gifting. My oldest son will celebrate a birthday, and I will clean my house. A lot.

It's only the third day of December, and I already feel hopelessly behind. Because this past Tuesday, on the very first day of this busiest of months, I received my first Christmas card. It's a lovely card, featuring pictures of dear friends and their beautiful, smiling children who are growing up too fast.

I do appreciate when friends take time out of their busy schedules to wish us well at the holidays. I'm just also a little jealous that they've marked card-sending off their list when I've barely gotten organized enough to include it on mine.

I have included it, though; and thanks to Sir Henry Cole, British civil servant, inventor, and all-around impressive guy, I'll get to it. By 1843, the tradition of handwriting special holiday greetings was well-established, but Cole was a busy man. He decided to take a shortcut and commissioned his friend, painter John Calcott Horsely, to design a commercial card. Cole ordered a thousand of them, sent some to his list, and sold the rest for six cents apiece.

The move was not without controversy. The more religiously zealous of the day declared the design a war on Christmas because in addition to images of service to the poor, it portrayed holiday merrymaking. And I'm sure there were a disappointed few who'd have preferred hand-painted burlap evergreens and artistically arranged lettering.

But Cole didn't let the naysayers get him down. Over the next few years, the commercial Christmas card market soared. Though it's waned somewhat with the increase in electronic forms of communication, it seems (from a random sampling of my mailbox) the tradition is still alive and well.

I wish my friends and family could expect hand-painted burlap evergreens and artistically arranged lettering, but they probably know better. I'm sure I will receive a few such lovingly crafted greetings, and I may feel a twinge of guilt for sending commercially produced cards.

Still, I will get around to sending a holiday greeting of some sort. It might feature controversial Christmas merrymaking. It will likely include a picture of my beautiful smiling children who are growing up too fast.

And there's almost definitely a very small chance it will even arrive before the new year.

December 10, 2015

That's How it Could Have Happened

It all started with a dinner party. In the early 1940s, musician Anthony Pratt made his living performing concerts at hotels throughout the English countryside. The popular evening entertainment of the day was dinner and a murder mystery.

In these live-action whodunits, actors and guests spread through the hotel, seeking clues to solve a murder. As guests answered questions about the murderer, crime scene, and weapon, it occurred to Pratt that he might have the makings of a board game.

He played around with the idea and in December of 1944, applied for a patent for his game "Murder!" In 1949, with a few tweaks, Pratt's game went into production with game manufacturer Waddingtons as "Cluedo." Simultaneously, Parker Brothers released the game in the United States, calling it "Clue." The game was a hit.

Then in December of 1985, Paramount released a film adaptation of it. All the brightly colored game characters arrive at a spooky mansion on a stormy night for a dinner party and a series of murders. The critical response to the film was more or less "meh." But audiences who had grown up playing Pratt's game liked it fine. The film developed a cult following proving to a curious world that Tim Curry looks better in a tuxedo than in women's lingerie.

I played the game Clue a lot when I was a kid. And though I didn't see the movie in the theater, it was one of my favorites. I watched it frequently on VHS, complete with all three possible endings and a load of pithy jokes. When our boys started enjoying the game, we showed them the movie, and they loved it, too.

So when a movie theater near our home screened Clue as part of a throwback film series, we geeked out. We rearranged our schedules, grabbed our tickets, and stayed out late on a school night to see it.

It was totally worth it. The catchy score was louder, the old mansion was creepier, and the growling guard dogs were scarier. With a large crowd laughing along, even the pithy jokes were funnier. Of course it didn't hurt that between handfuls of butter-soaked popcorn, my youngest was reciting right along with every line.

His favorite part occurs during the first ending in which Wadsworth the butler reveals that Miss Scarlet is the murderer. The two of them debate whether any bullets remain in the revolver, with Wadsworth eventually wrestling it away from Scarlet. When he then accidentally fires it, the bullet severs the cord holding the large chandelier. The chandelier nearly falls on Colonel Mustard, engaged in recounting the fired shots on his fingers, taking him by complete surprise.

It didn't matter that my son already knew the scene because everything's better on the big screen. Though originally released to theaters with only one of three endings, this screening of the movie included all three. We watched and laughed and went home happy.

And that's how it could have happened.

But then, a couple weeks later came our turn to host a large crowd of neighbors for the annual Christmas party. After a lot of baking, cooking, arranging, and cleaning, we were just about ready for the party to begin. The wine glasses were lined up on the kitchen island, and my husband stood at the stove with the last of the food nearly ready. Guests were due to arrive in about fifteen minutes.

I washed and dried one last cooking pot, hung it on the iron pot rack/light fixture above the island, and walked out of the kitchen. I had just made it through the doorway when I heard a very scary noise.

I looked back to see my husband, miraculously uninjured, doing his best Colonel Mustard impression. Inches behind him, the pot rack had crashed onto the counter, shattering the wine glasses, sending shards of broken glass across the kitchen and dining room.

Soon after, the doorbell rang. My first instinct was to shout like Mrs. Peacock, "Oh, whoever it is, they gotta go away or they'll be killed." But instead, I took a shaky breath, opened the door, and explained our situation.

It was a little darker in the kitchen. We swept up a lot of glass. But in the end, we managed to have a really nice evening with some very understanding neighbors. And best of all, no one was killed. In the kitchen. With the pot rack.

On the Shelf of Rarely Used Things

In a dark, unfinished corner of my basement, there is a set of rough wooden shelves where we keep things we've nearly forgotten. The bottom two shelves are mostly crammed with recently refilled boxes of Christmas decorations. But the top shelf contains even less useful items. The soft case for my saxophone I haven't played in forever is there, along with some old computer parts waiting to be recycled someday.

And next to that sits a box that hasn't been opened in more than fifteen years. The box was stored at my parent's house for a while and then moved in with us when we had room for it. It's traveled halfway across the country and back, been a little beaten up along the way, and gathered plenty of dust; but still, it's remained sealed.

Because what it contains is something I will never use again. I won't get rid of it, either. At least not any time soon. What it contains is my ridiculously formal, white wedding gown.

I've been thinking about that box a lot this week, and not just because I saw it as I stuffed away the Christmas decorations; but because this past Saturday, I had the opportunity to join one of my nieces in her shopping quest for her own ridiculously formal wedding gown.

The bride will be getting married next fall on the east coast; and her mother (affectionately known as the momzilla) decided to plan a Midwest gathering of epic proportions this holiday season, so that Grandma and most of the aunts and female cousins could participate in wedding dress shopping.

It was a really sweet idea, inspired in part by TLC's *Say Yes to the Dress*, an inexplicably addictive show in which brides try on crazy expensive and ornate dresses that they will only wear once. And then everyone cries.

That's pretty much how it went, too. On the designated day, eleven of us (including the bride and the momzilla) descended on an already busy bridal shop filled with rack after rack of white gowns. We were the largest group there that day, even causing the consultants a bit of grief as they lined up chairs around an elevated platform, where the bride would emerge from her dressing room.

At the momzilla's insistence, my niece tried on at least six gowns (this was an actual momzilla-issued mandate). Then she tried on just one more, one that wasn't anything like she had imagined she wanted. And we all cried. Seriously, it happened just like it does in the show. She tried on lots of beautiful white gowns, and she looked lovely in all of them; but this was clearly THE DRESS. The scene could have been scripted.

There's a look that comes over a bride, a certain expression that signals to everyone watching that she is suddenly able to envision it all; even if she didn't know it, this is the wedding dress she'd been picturing herself in. And once she's decided, there's very little chance of persuading her otherwise.

Perhaps that's what it was like for Queen Victoria when she broke with tradition in 1840 and donned a white gown covered in delicate English lace for her wedding to Prince Albert. Very few brides were wearing white at the time, but Victoria knew what she wanted. I imagine the first time she saw herself in that big, white dress, she got that look and cried. She also started a trend.

Ten years later, most wealthy English brides chose white gowns, and *Godey's Lady's Book*, the 19th-century American woman's go-to guide for all things fashionable, had this to say about wedding gowns: "Custom has decided, from the earliest ages, that white is the most fitting hue...It is an emblem of purity and innocence of girlhood, and the unsullied heart she now yields to the chosen one."

In the world of fashion, I guess ten years ago probably is considered the earliest ages; but whether the custom was long-standing then or not, it certainly is now. More than 90 percent of today's American brides wear white on their wedding days.

I suppose it's practical enough, if you plan to never wear the dress again and just have it cleaned and vacuum sealed into a box that you'll put up on the basement shelf of things you rarely use, until the daughter you may or may not have rejects it in favor of THE DRESS she saw in *Modern Bride Magazine*.

But that was one tradition Queen Victoria didn't start. In an era when most brides simply wore their best dress and then wore it again, Victoria re-wore her veil for christenings and other important life events, and she re-purposed bits of the delicate lace.

Now my dress might be used again someday. I don't have daughters, but I have a lot more nieces; and maybe someday, there will be future daughters-in-law who might want to give it a try. But I'm not holding my breath. Because there's something magical about that moment when a bride sees herself in THE DRESS, the one that, even though she may not have known it, is the one she's imagined sealing up in a box to store forever in her basement on the shelf of rarely used things.

The Dark Days of Pinball: How I Nearly Took a Sledgehammer to a Snowman

Seventy-four years ago, on January 21, 1942, Fiorello La Guardia, then mayor of New York, finally got around to addressing what can only be described as a scourge on the good citizens of his city. Long before loosie cigarette vendors and giant cups of killer soda, New York still had its fair share of problems. The biggest one of all was pinball.

Mayor La Guardia wasn't having it. "Pinball," he explained while gesturing wildly, "is a racket dominated by interests heavily tainted with criminality." He issued a directive to the NYC police department, expressing that the rounding up of pinball machines throughout the city was to be their top priority.

Over the course of a few weeks, police raided seedy pinball establishments, confiscating more than 3,000 machines. Then the mayor himself, a grand politician, took a few highly publicized swings at them with a sledgehammer, smashing them to bits.

Time and resources well spent, I'd say. But then I've never been very good at pinball, a game of some skill and a lot of luck.

And right now, I feel as if I've been playing it for the last three days. We had a long weekend this past weekend, with Martin Luther King Day on Monday and an additional teacher inservice training day for our school district on Tuesday.

My sons are 11 and 8, close enough in age to be really good friends and also terrible enemies, sometimes in the very same moment. So while we all enjoy the occasional break from school, it can start to feel like an elaborate game of pinball.

Everything is going along fine. Their imaginations are running wild, and they're having fun. Then they get bored. They fight. Someone ends up crying. I start yelling. I take a deep breath, pull back the spring loaded pin of creativity, and launch them an idea—something new to try, a game to play, a project to work on, a friend to call, or a book to read. It works for a little while. Enthusiastic and hopeful, they bounce off the walls, and I rack up a few creative mom points. Until they get bored. They fight. And someone ends up crying.

By the end of the day on Tuesday, I had pretty much exhausted every idea I ever had for keeping them busy. We were on the brink of something terrible. And that's when it started to snow.

The call came around 10:00 that night. The boys were tucked in and sleeping, and I was just beginning to relax, unwinding from the woes of the day before heading to bed myself when we received notice there would be no school the next day.

I love my children; but when I thought about spending another day of launching creative ideas at them only to wind up with one (or all) of us in tears, I was ready to whack a snowman with a sledgehammer.

That's kind of where Mayor La Guardia was at, too.

Because he'd already spent years trying to clean up his city. He'd taken on crime, ridding the city of the slot machines that funneled gambling money to the mafia.

And then the criminals launched pinball onto the scene. At the time, the game didn't yet include flippers and so involved much more chance than skill, pilfering, according to the mayor, "nickels and dimes given [children] as lunch money."

He wasn't alone in his crusade against the game. Cities across the US joined in the fight and banned pinball, sending it into the even deeper recesses of the shady underground, where only the most hardened of criminals could find it.

New York's ban lasted until 1976, when a heated pinball-focused city council hearing ended in a spectacular demonstration of skill by Roger Sharpe, by day a respected young magazine editor and by night a hardened pinball criminal from New York's seedy underbelly.

Sharpe played for a bit with mixed reviews; and then in one final attempt to impress, he called a difficult launch and delivered. The city council immediately declared that pinball was more than a game of mere chance, and the ban was lifted.

Fortunately, school is in session today; but if it weren't, I'd have had to institute a ban on creative mom pinball. I'd have been making a few highly skilled calls myself, frantically launching my boys toward the homes of friends or grandparents. Because if they'd been home with me again today, I'm pretty sure I would have taken out a few snowmen with a sledgehammer.

Just Please Don't Tell My Husband

When I got married, more than 15 years ago now, my mother gave me some sage advice. "Sarah," she said, "whatever he's really good at, you let him do it, and you never ever learn how." There's a great deal of wisdom in those words. Of course, she didn't mean for me to be helpless and to rely on my man to take care of all the big stuff. What she meant was twofold:

1. It's important to build your partner up and let him know his contribution to even the simple things in your relationship is valuable.

2. If you do that consistently, then you will never have to do the cooking on chili night.

My dad does make a mean pot of chili, and he has a few other signature dishes, too. And somehow Mom can't manage to master any of them. But I'll let you (and my dad since he reads this blog) in on a little secret. She's a pretty competent cook and probably could make chili if she had a mind to. (Sorry, Mom, but after 50+ years, I suspect he already knows anyway).

I have a lot of respect for my mother, for both my parents, and for their long-lasting marriage, so I have done my best to follow this advice. But this week, my determination to do so has been tested. Because this past Tuesday was Pancake Day.

For many of my American readers, you may not realize that that's how much of the world refers to what we tend to call Mardi Gras or Fat Tuesday or Shrove Tuesday. It's the day before Ash Wednesday, that marks the end of the upbeat season of Epiphany and the eve of the somber season of Lent on the Christian calendar.

Because Lent is observed as a season of repentance and often of denial of the flesh, Shrove Tuesday developed, probably in the Middle Ages, as a day of feasting in order to consume perishable foods that would not be eaten during the next 40 days leading up to Easter.

Flour, milk, and fats needed to be used up. To the English, that sounded like a good reason to whip up a batch of pancakes. According to legend, in 1445 in Olney in Buckinghamshire, one woman did just that. But she didn't have very good timing because when the bell rang out to announce the beginning of the church service of confession (or shriving service), she was right in the middle of cooking her pancakes. A devout woman, she dashed off to church anyway, arriving breathless in her apron with her frying pan in hand.

In her honor, the Olney pancake race has become a famous annual Pancake Day tradition, featuring women (or men in drag), running a 415-yard course toward the church while carrying a hot pancake in a pan. In order to win, a contestant must flip her pancake during the race a minimum of three times and arrive first to serve it, still hot, to the bell ringer.

There are a lot of Shrove Tuesday traditions observed the world over, but this is by far my favorite. Someday, I hope to participate.

And now I can because I very recently learned how to make pancakes. I realize they aren't terribly difficult to make, and it might be a little sad that a woman in her late thirties may not have known precisely how to do it; but what can I say?

I listen to my mother. And my husband makes amazing pancakes.

It has long been our family tradition that on Shrove Tuesday, we eat pancakes (made by my husband, of course, because I never have to do the cooking on pancake night). Unfortunately, this year he had to be out of town. I assumed that my sons and I would just go out to eat our traditional meal that evening. Until my oldest spiked a several-day fever and wasn't fit to go to school or to eat at a crowded restaurant.

Still, tradition is tradition, and so with trepidation, I took down the old family recipe book and looked up pancakes, a recipe, I might add, that is incomplete because my husband has tweaked it over the years.

According to my children, my pancakes didn't turn out too bad, though I hope they don't tell their dad. I'd like to think his title of official family pancake maker is safe. It's one skill I don't mind not perfecting, and there are plenty of other things I'm good at. In fact, according to my mother, I make the best blueberry muffins on the planet, a skill she just can't seem to master.

The Pizza of the Future: Naming of the Newest Planet X

For then 11-year-old Venetia Burney, March 14, 1930 started out very much like any normal day. She was eating breakfast with her mother and grandfather. Her grandfather, Falconer Madan (who in addition to having a cool name was a university librarian retired from Oxford), read out some exciting news from the morning paper.

Earlier that year, on February 18, an amazing discovery had been made by Lowell Observatory photographic telescope operator Clyde Tombaugh (who also had a pretty cool name). Detecting subtle differences between two photographs of the night sky, Tombaugh was able to zero in on an elusive body in space, a ninth planet known then as Planet X. Long believed to exist, this small, icy planet might have served as the explanation for the wonky orbital patterns of Uranus and Neptune.

But one question remained. Madan wondered aloud what the new ninth planet would be called. Young Venetia thought for a moment and told her grandfather that as the other planets were named after Roman gods (the exception being Uranus because that's just comedy gold), then this new planet should be Pluto.

Like any good grandfather, Madan thought his granddaughter was brilliant. So he contacted an astronomer friend, who passed it along to the research team at Lowell Observatory in Arizona, who announced the official name of the ninth planet in our solar system on May 1, 1930.

For 76 years, everyone was happy. The smallest, little, underdog planet in the solar system, discovered by a non-college-educated, amateur astronomer plucked from obscurity because of his enthusiasm and named by a clever 11-year-old girl, captured human imagination. Even Mickey Mouse named his best friend after the plucky, little ice planet, and generations of school children remembered its name because of the mnemonic: My Very Educated Mother Just Served Us Nine Pizzas.

And everybody loves pizza. Except for Caltech astronomer Mike Brown (who has a very common name), also known as the man who killed Pluto. I have to assume his mother never brought him any pizza. I admit that like many (okay, probably all) amateur astronomy enthusiasts, I was a little miffed with Brown for a while. I like Pluto.

But I understand how science works. I understand that the most plausible idea is only the truth until it isn't. I can accept that Brown and all those other backstabbing, planet-murdering scientists who voted in 2006 to demote my favorite non-Earth planet to dwarf status probably had a point.

And in January of this year, Brown softened the blow, when he and fellow Caltech researcher Konstantin Batygin (another super cool name) announced that they may have discovered the real mystery planet behind the wonky orbital patterns of Uranus and Neptune and the ring of icy debris and dwarf planets that include Pluto.

I don't really expect this new, much larger planet (it's about 10 times the size of Earth) to replace Pluto in my affections. And since today is the 86th anniversary of the discovery of our original number nine, I plan to remember it fondly. But I will watch with interest as Brown and Batygin attempt to verify this new planet's presence via telescope over the next few years.

I suppose when they do, it will need an extremely cool name. I hope they leave that part up to the clever 11-year-olds out there, who are bound to choose a name that begins with P. Because everyone likes pizza. And I can't wait to celebrate by serving nine of them.

February 25, 2016

The Longest Shortest Month Ever

In 46 BC, just a couple years before the arrogant and power-hungry Roman Emperor Julius Caesar had a really bad day in mid March, he decided to tackle the problem of the Roman calendar. Before then, years were measured by lunar cycle, a system that led to the need for the occasional addition of an extra month and frankly, confused the heck out of everyone.

Consulting with Egyptian astronomer Sosigenes, Caesar learned that it would make a great deal more sense to measure a year as 365 days, add a leap day every fourth year, and rename one of the twelve months (July) in honor of himself; because when you've managed to get yourself declared "emperor perpetuity" of a republic (as every fan of *Star Wars* and/or history knows), you can do pretty much whatever you want to.

Even though the calendar was still a little off (about 11 minutes every year) and would eventually be revised by Pope Gregory XIII (which also confused the heck out of everyone), the concept is still used today. And that's why this stupid February, which has been a stressful one at our house, will be one stupid day longer this year.

Okay, so it might not actually be February's fault; but all I know is that in January, everyone in my family was in perfect health. Then with the new month came the crud. My oldest was the first victim. He missed nearly a week of school because of fever and respiratory symptoms (No, not the flu. And yes, we vaccinate.) This week, it struck my younger son. And in between, it hit me.

Now, when kids are sick, we obviously do what we need to do. We keep them home from school, entrenched on the couch with a box of tissues, a bottle of Gatorade, and a stack of movies. We pile on the blankets, monitor temperatures, and fret over medication schedules. We rub backs, kiss foreheads, and soothe heartache over missed activities.

That's all well and good. But when Mom gets sick, it's different. Because even at home, there are still things that must be taken care of. This is likely the reason that I have been symptomatic at least five days longer than son # 1 was, and why my own battle with the crud, though it started almost a week earlier, has lasted well into that of son #2.

It really was beginning to look like I might cough and hack my way to the very end of this stupid month. Fortunately, I married a wise man, who I finally decided to listen to (possibly because I couldn't talk for all the coughing). He insisted that I take a day off.

Now, I work from home, which means taking a day off can be tricky because I'm pretty much always at work. But he was clear. No dishes and no laundry (no problem so far) and no writing. Wait. What?

One day of rest, both physical and mental.

My youngest son was still home, so I did have to see to his needs. But it turned out, his disappointment at having to miss another day of school and activities was somewhat soothed by the idea that Mom was in it with him. We piled up the blankets, shared a big box of tissues, and settled in for a day of movie watching.

By the next day, we both felt a lot better. He headed off to school. I headed back to my computer, healthier and wiser and grateful that the end of this longest shortest month ever is finally in sight. No, February is not my favorite month with its cold, dreary days, but it's still short even when it's long; and I suppose this year, I should be thankful it has a built-in sick day.

March 24, 2016

A Spring Break Disappearing Act

This week, my children have been on Spring Break, a time of staying up late, sleeping in, and generally making their mother panic about how to fill the many hours of a rapidly approaching summer break. At this point in their academic careers, it's also a time for them to set aside school projects in favor of more leisurely passions.

For my first born son, a bright 11-year-old, that means magic. I'm not actually sure when this latest obsession began to take root, but for months he's been studying library books full of sleight of hand techniques and grand illusions. My basement is filled with discarded attempts at fashioning a cardboard vanishing cabinet. He has even worked hard to design schemes that can convince an audience of his psychic abilities.

This last one is pretty easy to unravel as he always recruits his little brother to be his less-than-subtle audience plant. Still, I'm reasonably confident that if he sticks with it, he will eventually figure out how to pull off some convincing illusions.

In fact, he's already managed a few fairly impressive card tricks that I have a hard time figuring out. It's these he's worked on the most, mastering some classics and tweaking a few to make them his own. Now I'm thinking the book he might really need to read is what has become known as the "Card Sharp Bible," *The Expert at the Card Table: The Classic Treatise on Card Manipulation* by S. W. Erdnase.

Originally published by James McKinney and Co. in Chicago in 1902, this little book has been in continuous print for over 100 years and is widely considered the most influential book on card manipulation ever written.

Erdnase's work includes 16 techniques of blind shuffles and card cutting with illustrations. Bottom dealing, deck stacking, and second dealing are all thoroughly explained. There are discussions of card palming, sleight of hand illusions, and plain old card tricks.

But the most impressive trick tackled by Erdnase is the author's own disappearing act because even after more than 100 years and numerous exhaustive searches, no one is quite sure of the author's true identity. We know only that S. W. Erdnase is a pseudonym (understandable given the potentially illegal applications of the subject matter in his book) and that the author sold his rights to the book a year after it was originally published.

There's been A LOT of speculation about who he might have been. From an interview conducted 40 years later with the original illustrator, we have a vague description of a short, well-spoken, and pleasant man, who may have mentioned a familial connection to political cartoonist Louis Dalrymple.

It's not a lot to go on, but clever investigators quickly latched onto the fact that S. W. Erdnase is the backwards spelling of E. S. Andrews. This has led to a number of potential candidates and dead ends, including a notorious Chicago conman by that name and a Herbert Andrews, whose business was located a few blocks from the book's publisher and whose wife was Emma Shaw Andrews.

Other clever investigators have put forward the suggestion of successful mining engineer W. E. Sanders, whose name anagrams nicely into S. W. Erdnase. Still others have proposed Peruvian magician L'Homme Masque, whose prowess in the magic community at the time might at least recommend him as a contributor or Harry S. Thompson, a salesman who was both a short, well-spoken man and a friend to Harry Houdini.

The debate rages on, but it seems unlikely that the true *Expert at the Card Table* will ever reappear. The real question, it seems, is how he managed to so completely vanish in the first place. Personally, I'm betting it had something to do with a vanishing cabinet, made of cardboard, in his mother's basement.

This Truly Tragic Streetlamp

Yesterday was leftover day at my house. Actually, it's pretty much been leftover week. Because whenever we host a major holiday, we somehow wind up with all the food. Everyone comes with full hands and empty stomachs and then leaves with full stomachs and empty hands.

I don't mind exactly. We have a family full of wonderful, generous people, a very good "problem" to have; and I kind of like the challenge of figuring out how to creatively use up all the leftovers. After this Easter Sunday, we were left with a refrigerator full of ham and turkey and deviled eggs and potato salad and vegetable tian and roasted carrots. We also had brownies and fruit salad and rolls.

And we had four people, at least one of whom rarely eats anything.

So when my boys asked yesterday what I was making for dinner, I responded by sharing my very clever plan to make a turkey pot pie to use up the last of the bird and most of the remaining vegetables. It was genius, really, a dish both tasty and useful.

But the protests I got over my cleverness were swift and furious and unrelenting. You'd think I'd made a proposal that would forever alter the food landscape of our home, perhaps permanently damaging our otherwise perfectly developed palates. I admit I wasn't prepared for such resistance.

I wondered if this was how Alexandre-Gustave Eiffel felt when in February of 1887, 300 of Paris's most influential artistic minds came together to launch a very loud complaint. Addressed to Charles Alphand, Minister of Works and Commissioner for the 1889 World's Fair, and printed in the newspaper *Le Temps*, the complaint stated:

We, writers, painters, sculptors, architects, passionate lovers of the beauty, until now intact, of Paris, hereby protest with all our might, with all our indignation, in the name of French taste gone unrecognized, in the name of French art and history under threat, against the construction, in the very heart of our capital, of the useless and monstrous Eiffel Tower.

The statement went on from there, but it's safe to say that the additional words were in no way flattering to the project then already underway to construct a centerpiece for the upcoming World Exposition, which would commemorate 100 years of the French Republic.

And at first, Alexandre-Gustave Eiffel might have agreed with the complaints. When two of his company's senior engineers, Maurice Koechlin and Émile Nouguier, first presented a design proposal for a "great pylon, consisting of four lattice girders standing apart at the base and coming together at the top, joined together by metal trusses at regular intervals," Eiffel wasn't wild about it.

But when the two engineers pulled in architect Stephen Sauvestre to add a few decorative arches and a little flare, Eiffel began to see the possibilities. Suddenly, what he was looking at was a kind of sexy pylon, consisting of four lattice girders standing apart at the base and coming together at the top, joined by metal trusses at regular intervals. Much better.

And he argued, such a large, tall structure would be a

potentially useful tool in scientific studies in astronomy, meteorology, aerodynamics, and communications. In a rebuttal to the artists' protest, he asked, "Is it not true that the very conditions which give strength also conform to the hidden rules of harmony?" He continued by pointing to the many considerations necessary for creating functional art on a large scale and in the end, concluded that while engineers rule, artists drool.

It took some time, but by March 31, 1889, when Eiffel climbed 1,710 steps to unfurl the French flag from what he identified as the longest flagpole in all the nations of the world, some of the original 300 protesters had come around to thinking the tower was kind of neat. And soon enough, they were setting up their easels and trying to sell paintings of it to the more than 7 million annual tourists that flock to this most visited monument in the world.

I wish I could say my own experiment in monumentally clever leftover use was as successful. I didn't listen to my protesters either, but I didn't give them any witty arguments about how perhaps the most artistic dishes are those that are delicious, nutritious, and practical all at the same time. I simply reminded them that dinner was already planned and that I don't get to be called "Mom" for nothing.

The pot pie was pretty good. My sons will never know that because they didn't eat it. But I have a surprise for them. There're still plenty of leftovers, so tonight I'm planning to make a quiche. I know it will be a monumental success that may even become a legendary symbol of our home. Or more likely, they won't eat it. But they'll still have to call me Mom.

April 21, 2016

The Greatest Post Since Sliced Bread

On January 18, 1943, the head of the War Food Administration, Claude R. Wickard, instituted a ban on the sale of sliced bread in the United States. It was a move that didn't make him a lot of friends. His claim was that by halting the manufacture of steel bread slicing machines, a lot of steel could be preserved for the war effort. Of course, the argument doesn't really hold up when one considers the fairly slow rate of production for such machines, having been in wide use in bakeries ever since their invention 14 years earlier sparked an enthusiastic love affair between Americans and pre-sliced bread.

But besides just the not-so-significant steel savings, banning sliced bread also offered the advantage of lowering demand for bread, thereby counteracting the 10% increase in wheat prices instituted by the Office of Price Administration in an effort to preserve wheat stores. At the time, said stores included only enough to meet normal US consumption for an entire two years without any additional harvest.

Still, there's the very real concern that sliced bread staled faster than its non-sliced counterpart. Because of this, Food and Drug Administration regulations required the use of a thicker waxed paper for its packaging. And despite the fact that paper manufacturers and bakers easily had a four month supply already on hand at the time the ban went into effect, everyone knows that a military that runs low on waxed paper isn't a military that can win a war.

Perhaps not surprisingly, the American public, which was generally pretty understanding about sacrificing for the good of the war effort, didn't think much of Wickard's ban. One righteously angry housewife explained in a *New York Times* article that between packing lunches and serving breakfast to her husband and four children, she had to quickly hand-slice 22 pieces of bread every morning. Sliced bread, she insisted, was essential to the "morale and saneness of a household."

Other women were simply left bewildered, consulting bread slicing instruction sheets given out by local bakeries, including such helpful advice as: "Keep your head down. Keep your eye on the loaf. Don't bear down." Soft as they had become by the easy luxury of pre-sliced bread, it's a wonder most housewives didn't cut off any of their own fingers.

It's amazing, really, to think how important this one product became to the American public. In just 14 years, from its humble beginnings at the Chillicothe Baking Company in Chillicothe, Missouri, where jeweler and determined inventor Otto Rohwedder introduced his bread slicing machine to a dubious public, sliced bread rose to its essential morale-boosting status, as the greatest thing since, well, whatever great thing came before sliced bread, I guess.

And there can be little doubt that the ill-considered ban on it was one of the dumber moves of the War Food Administration. The ban was lifted less than two months later, well before the sliced bread industry would have even come close to burning through its stockpile of FDA-approved thick waxed paper. To the vindicated public, a sheepish Wickard admitted, "The savings are not as much as expected."

Now, I have to say I buy my share of bakery-fresh bread,

unsliced, both because fresh bread tastes delicious and the idea of the load of preservatives required to replace the extra-thick waxed paper once used to extend shelf-life kind of gives me a case of the willies. Still, I understand the struggle eloquently expressed by the woman in the *New York Times*. When I'm slapping sandwiches together to stuff into lunchboxes every morning, it lifts my spirits to be able to reach for a twisty-tied bag of sliced bread without having to break the law.

It turns out after the War Food Administration lifted its ban, the good guys went on to win World War II anyway. They did it even against incredible odds resulting from the looming possible hint of maybe a slight waxed paper shortage. And they did it, a practical historian might argue, as a direct result of the morale boost of having sliced bread for their sandwiches.

April 28, 2016

A Bear with no Face and a Clean-Shaven Pharaoh

When we moved into our current house a little more than three years ago, we gained more than a new home and a lovely new set of neighbors. We also got a new family mascot. A wooden bear guarded our front walk, carved from half a log, so that it appeared as if his bottom portion was tucked down inside a hollowed out stump.

Though it was perhaps not something we would have chosen ourselves, we admired the craftsmanship, and our bear quickly became just one of those quirky things that made our new house our home. So I was a little sad when about a year after we moved in, my youngest son came inside one day to tell me that through no fault of his own, the bear's snout had fallen clean off its face.

I wasn't exactly shocked at the news. We knew the bear had been around a while. The previous homeowners had left it obviously, but we suspected they weren't the first. Over the years, our bear had grown a nice crop of lichen, provided ample wood pulp for a slew of paper wasps, and had added a fair bit of rotted off bark to our landscaping. He honestly wasn't in the greatest of shape when we found him.

When my husband got home that evening, he shrugged

and secured the poor bear's snout back on his head with a nice, big screw through the middle of its nose. It wasn't a perfect fix, but we still had a bear; and from a distance, it worked.

For a while.

I would hope that the staff of Cairo's Egyptian Museum, which houses more than 120,000 artifacts from Egyptian antiquity, would have a slightly less cavalier attitude when their most famous artifact, the 3,300 year-old death mask of Tutankhamun, lost its beard.

It happened during part of routine maintenance performed by museum staff in August of 2014. This wasn't the first time King Tut had gone clean shaven. When Howard Carter opened the young pharaoh's innermost coffin on October 28, 1925, the beard, previously attached to the mask with beeswax, had come loose. In 1944, it was secured in place with wooden dowels and eventually solder.

But when it came loose again in 2014, the panicked museum staff, evidently concerned about the effect of taking arguably the world's most recognized Egyptian artifact off exhibit, decided to fix it. Fast. They applied a quick-drying epoxy, scraping off the extra with a spatula that left a mark. It wasn't a perfect fix, but they still had a golden death mask and from a distance, it worked.

For a while.

But pretty soon pictures began to surface that showed a clearly visible yellow glue ringing King Tut's beard, and three anonymous curators came clean to the press.

Fortunately, there's a happy ending to the story. After much angst, a team of restoration experts managed to remove the damaging epoxy residue and attached the pharaoh's royal facial hair with beeswax, just as the original artists did. Though there still may be some legal entanglements for some of the parties originally involved in the hasty repair and cover-up, the mask is once again on public display, as good as old.

I wish I could say the same for the fate of our bear. After a few more months, the reattached snout became too decayed to hold into place with the screw. For a long time, lacking a replacement and unwilling to go without, a bear with no face stood guard over our front walk. Then a couple weeks ago, I stumbled on another bear. It's not handcrafted or as nice as our first bear probably originally was. But it has a face, so it'll do.

Now I realize that on the scale of significant works of art, our old guard bear has nowhere near the importance to the world that the death mask of King Tut does. I was, nonetheless, sad to see him go. On a still, somber evening last weekend, we lit a bonfire and said a respectful goodbye.

Almost 43 Quintillion Ways Not to Solve a Rubik's Cube

On May 19, 1974, a Hungarian professor of architecture figured out how to build just the right model to aid in teaching algebraic group theory to his students. The model was a cube, composed of 26 smaller cubes that could freely rotate around one another without falling apart.

And the model was useful, but there was a small problem. Because once the professor started moving the individual cubes, he quickly realized that what he really had on his hands was a pretty great puzzle that even he wasn't sure how to solve.

It took Professor Erno Rubik over a month to sort out the solution to his wonderful new puzzle toy, which could be rearranged in 43 quintillion different ways. Now, personally I find his success pretty impressive; but given that the current world record for solving a single 3 x 3 Rubik's Cube is a cool 4.9 seconds and that a little girl who was not yet three did it unofficially on the Internet in 70 seconds, it's maybe a little embarrassing.

But no other toy has captured the imagination of the world in quite the same way as the Rubik's Cube. It quickly became the most popular toy in Hungary in the late 70s; and when it launched onto the international scene in 1980, it became a defining image of a decade.

As of this time last year, Rubik's Cube remains the single best-selling toy of all time with over 350 million cubes sold, at least .0004% of which have been solved. The rest have either been pulled apart with pliers, had their stickers removed, or been simply left for dead under a heavy piece of furniture.

Because the majority of us haven't made it through all 43 quintillion possibilities yet in order to solve it. I admit, I was one of those kids who was never able to do it; and it's possible I may have pulled off a sticker or two in an attempt to return it to its pristine state (which doesn't work very well). And so, I was never a big fan.

But I am a big fan of the Internet and YouTube, responsible most recently for teaching me important skills like how to tie a bow tie (which I can do, like a boss) and how to make a terrific balsamic chicken (which not surprisingly, my children will not eat). So, a few years ago, I decided to recruit some Internet help and finally solve my Rubik's Cube problem. After all, if a mantis shrimp can solve the puzzle (It can't. Don't believe everything you see on YouTube.), then surely I can.

And I did. No, really, I did. I followed the instructions very carefully, and I messed it up. A lot. I threw my cube across the room several times. And I started again. And I eventually got it to work out. It took me a little longer than 4.9 seconds, but shorter than a month.

True story.

Of course anyone who has ever owned a Rubik's Cube (and there's a 1 in 7 chance that includes you) knows that you can't just leave it done. Those colors call to you. They just have to be scrambled; and no matter how much you resist, it will always happen.

So, I thought, just for the purpose of this blog post, I would give it another go. I'd done it once. How hard could it be?

Um, the answer to that is HARD. Like, really hard. I think I watched the official Rubik's Cube solving guide videos somewhere in the neighborhood of 43 quintillion times before I threw the cube across the room, where it disappeared under a heavy piece of furniture.

But as Erno Rubik once famously said, "If you are curious, you'll find the puzzles around you. If you are determined, you will solve them." So, I think I'll stick with it. I'll solve it again someday. That is if I can ever find it.

August 25, 2016

Man-Bats and Bipedal Moon Beavers

January 10, 1834 was a remarkable day in the history of humankind. It was the day Sir John Herschel, a noted English astronomer and son of William Herschel, the discoverer of Uranus, first gazed through his super-powered telescope and observed life on the moon.

The account of his wondrous findings first appeared in the *Edinburgh Journal of Science*; but since obviously no one reads scientific journals, the story didn't really take off until a more layman-friendly version written by Herschel's colleague, Dr. Andrew Grant, appeared as a series of feature articles in the *New York Sun* penny newspaper, beginning August 25, 1835.

The articles started with a thorough description of Herschel's unique telescope and continued over the course of the next five issues to describe details of landscape, plant life, and numerous animal species, including unicorns, herds of moon bison, spherical amphibians, bipedal beavers, and winged human-like creatures dubbed *Vespertilio-homo*, or man-bat.

The sixth and final installment detailed a superior example of *Vespertilio-homo*, which engaged in the most civilized of activities in close proximity to a structure that appeared to be a sapphire temple. Then it went on to explain that as the scientists took a break to discuss their findings, they accidentally left the lens of the high-powered telescope directed toward the sun and burned down a portion of the observatory. Sadly, by the time repairs were made, the moon was no longer in a position conducive to further observation.

Now, as an intelligent reader of all true things on the Internet, you may have begun to realize by now that this story that really did run in the *New York Sun* might not have been entirely factual. But the readers of the *Sun* were somewhat less sophisticated than the ~~average~~ discerning readers of today. And there was just enough truth to the story to make it sound kind of plausible to those who weren't really paying attention, including a fair number of scientists who were thrilled by the discovery.

For example, it is true that Sir John Herschel traveled to South Africa in January of 1834 with a powerful telescope. It's true, also, that the scientific community of the day was still somewhat divided on whether or not life on the moon could be possible. Herschel himself had not yet come down on one side or the other of the issue.

It's true, too, that there had been, at one time, an *Edinburgh Journal of Science*, and that no one read it. Or at least no one had read it in the several years leading up to the *Sun* article because it had ceased to be in print. And when one considers that pretty much every sane person believed in roaming herds of moon unicorns, it's not hard to see why everyone got so excited.

But there was no such person as Dr. Andrew Grant. He was likely an invention of reporter Richard Adams Locke. He never actually claimed responsibility for writing the articles, possibly because as a former editor of the work of Edgar Allan Poe, there's a pretty good chance Locke plagiarized the whole story from Poe's *The Unparalleled Adventures of One Hans Pfaall*.

But wherever it came from, the story was a huge success.

Some readers were skeptical, of course, but they tweeted about it and shared the stories to their Facebook walls all the same. And within little more than a month, the story had been picked up and repeated so many times, news of it had travelled all the way to Europe, where, to the credit of the European media, it was known most often as a silly American hoax.

The *New York Sun* did admit to the hoax eventually, but there was no retraction; and with the exception of the editor of its biggest competitor, who was probably just bitter he hadn't thought of it himself, no one seemed to care all that much. Even Sir John Herschel mostly just found the whole thing amusing. After a while he did get a little tired of answering questions about it in the middle of his very serious and important scientific lectures that no one was really listening to anyway. Still, questions about the hoax were preferable to the standard, "So," snort, giggle, giggle, "has your dad looked at Uranus lately?"

And so the world went on, bipedal moon beavers and man-bats once again became the stuff of legend, and journalism and perhaps humankind in general continued down a very slippery slope. These days reporters can't remember whether or not their helicopters were shot down, politicians may become confused about their own well-documented heritages, and overwhelming evidence of perjury isn't always enough to pursue charges. Really, in the grand scheme of lies, the Moon Hoax isn't so bad.

On the Origin of Clutter by Means of Accidental Collection, or the Preservation of Favoured Artwork in the Struggle for Back to School Organization

Finally, a new school year has begun for my children. For the most part, it's going well. My youngest loves his teacher. She seems warm and genuine and well organized, which is a great place to start. My older son is now navigating the halls of middle school, where he has so far managed to remember his locker combination and land in classes taught by teachers as wonderfully quirky as he is. I suppose it takes a special kind of crazy to teach middle schoolers.

What this all means for me is that I am a more or less full-time writer again, and that's going okay, too. In the five days they've been back at school, I've managed to draft several short stories and prep a good chunk of the first draft of a novel for the impending painful process of substantial revision.

But I've also had to take a little time to get my space organized for long days alone in front of the computer. I work in a little hidey hole of a room tucked down a dark hallway in my basement, a place where sometimes the dog even forgets to look for me.

I like having this space, but it can feel a little dismal at times, especially since it often becomes the staging area not just for my writing, but for my organizing as well. Like, for instance, when it came time to buy school supplies a few weeks ago, I started by sorting through the supplies from last year that had been unceremoniously dumped from backpacks on the floor of the closet of my hidey hole. The backpacks were there, too.

Also there were the remains of art projects and reports and poems and notes and all the precious little papers from a year of school that a mom can't quite bring herself to throw out. And maybe a few from previous years as well.

Okay, I admit, it was my New Year's resolution to pare down on the clutter; but in my defense, I also have yet to lose that pesky ten pounds. Actually, I've done fairly well sorting through and throwing away or donating my own stuff. With the kiddos, it's always a little harder. I think it's safe to say I'm not alone in this because even Charles Darwin struggled when it came to throwing out the artsy creations of his children.

We know because in 2003, Cambridge University and the American Museum of Natural History launched a collaborative effort to digitize all of Darwin's writings and make them available online. The project is ongoing, but currently includes more than 23,000 digital images. This is pretty cool if you're interested in getting to know the man behind one of the most influential (and contentious) scientific theories of all time.

But the coolest part to me is the handful of remaining pages of original handwritten text from *On the Origin of Species by Means of Natural Selection, or the Preservation of Favoured Races in the Struggle for Life*. Man, was he good with a title! There are only about 30 or so of these pages still in existence, and at least some of them are probably still around because a young Darwin artist or two drew on the backs of them.

The collection includes more than 50 examples of the Darwin children's drawings and stories, all preserved on what the evidently thrifty Charles Darwin must have considered scrap paper, not realizing that his handwritten notes and papers might one day be of interest to posterity.

What it seems he did realize is that in addition to being the man behind the theory that lit the field of natural science on fire, he was also a father of some pretty great kids; and their contribution to his life's work wasn't something he could part with.

As I work my way through the clutter and get settled back into my hidey hole, I realize I'm not going to be able to throw out those little bits of creativity either. I haven't come up with any great scientific theories (yet), and I doubt very much that the mess from the floor of my office closet will ever be catalogued and digitized for the benefit of the world. But if I'm wrong, everyone will know that I'm the mother of some pretty great kids.

September 22, 2016

Twenty Years of Fillin' Up Dates

It was 1896 when young office worker Artie Blanchard met the love of his life. He spotted Mamie at a casual dance on North Clark Street and recruited the guy next to him to be his on-the-spot wingman. Impressed with Artie's wit, Mamie gave him the chance he was looking for, and they had their first date, right there on the dance floor.

Of course, they didn't call it a date at the time because no one did. In fact, the thing itself was still a pretty novel concept. With a swelling of immigration into American cities, what had long been a somewhat public event carried out in the parlor or on the front porch swing under the careful supervision of parents was in the process of morphing into something new. Courtship was becoming dating.

And no one had quite decided yet what to call it. That is, until Artie came along. Though he and Mamie eventually decided to marry, the beginning of their relationship was a little rough, and at one point, she stopped seeing him entirely, preferring the company of another young man. Artie confronted her, saying, "Well, I s'pose the other boys fillin' all my dates?"

The scene occurs in *Artie: A Story of the Streets and Towns*, a series of columns written by American humorist George Ade that appeared in the *Chicago Record*. The series, like most of Ade's writings, takes a humorous look at the changing manners of the common working city dwellers, including a laugh-out-loud discussion of the intricacies of flirtatious communications, involving stamp placement, handkerchief manipulation, and how one chooses to hold an umbrella.

And if we can take the word of author Moira Weigel in her book *Labor of Love: The Invention of Dating* (and we probably should because odds are she did way more research than I did), Ade also coined the word "date," as it pertains to young men and women going out for dinner and a movie, or anonymously chatting one another up on a dating website, or swiping right, or whatever the cool kids are doing these days.

Because the typical first date has gone through a few changes since the early days of Artie and Mamie. And sometimes, a couple may even have a hard time retrospectively pinpointing exactly when that first date occurred.

In some ways, that's true of me and my husband, though this day is the anniversary we celebrate. Today, we have been together as a couple for 20 years. That's right, 20 YEARS! For those of you keeping track at home, I am not yet 40, which means we have been together for more than half of my life.

But what happened 20 years ago today wasn't probably a classic first date. We didn't go dancing or to the theater. We didn't grab a cup of coffee. He didn't swipe right, though I'm sure he would have if such a thing as Tinder had existed.

We were college students with mutual friends, and all of us tended to hang out in a group. On September 22, we were doing just that, when something that had already become obvious to our friends started to become obvious to us. You see, even though we liked being with all of our friends, what mattered most to each of us was that the other one was there. Something changed that day.

The next afternoon, we took a walk across campus, the first time we'd gone anywhere together alone. And maybe that was our real first date. I don't know.

What I do know is that 20 years, a happy marriage, and two kids later, we're still fillin' up one another's dates. And I suppose we have the eloquent George Ade and his somewhat less eloquent pal Artie to thank for it.

A Preview of

Smoke Rose to Heaven

A Novel by

Sarah Angleton

Coming fall of 2017 from

High Hill Press

Smoke Rose to Heaven

1872

The fortuneteller had forgotten about him by the time the man worked up the nerve to knock on her door. Ever a keen observer, she had spied him earlier in the evening. For hours he stood just across the street, rebuffing the advances of prostitutes and evading the notice of the roaming packs of drunken sailors looking for trouble. The man appeared respectable enough, tall and slender in a dull brown sack suit. Respectability was rare on Water Street and she assumed he must be a missionary.

She had been busy that evening with customers dropping in one after another. Several of the men she saw were newly arrived immigrants bound for work on the construction project for that ridiculous bridge to Brooklyn. Soon they would descend into the caisson that was described as the pit of hell and from which few men arose again unscathed. The workers came to her for hope, something she could not offer them. Even without the gift of supernatural sight she could see their fates far too clearly.

Bidding farewell to her last customer, she watched him stumble into the night before locking the door. Exhausted, she dropped into the seekers' chair to catch her breath and reflect on how even simple tasks had grown difficult. Then came the quiet yet insistent knocking at the door and she remembered the lurking, respectable man she'd seen outside earlier.

Opening the door, the fortuneteller sensed immediately that the man was in danger, just as certainly as she sensed the name by which he identified himself was not his own. What she failed to anticipate was that he would know her name.

"Pardon me, Madam, my name is Silas Allen. I'm looking for a woman by the name of Ada Powell." He paused, perhaps trying to read her expression, though the fortuneteller would reveal nothing. Undaunted by her stoicism, Mr. Allen continued, "Are you Ada Powell?"

His tentative speech failed to mask that his words were more statement than question. She drew a labored breath, cleared her throat, and motioned for him to take a seat at her table. Ada Powell was indeed the nearest she had to a true name, but she had not heard it in years. Ada took her own seat across the table from her visitor and examined him more closely before deciding how to respond. He was of middle age, with coarse features, wild brown hair, and dark, tired eyes. His broad shoulders and calloused hands suggested that he was no stranger to manual labor. His frayed coat was clean, his white shirt, crisp and fresh. He slumped slightly in the chair, a weary soul and, Ada decided, one who meant her no harm.

"Mr. Allen," Ada began, careful not to betray her apprehension. "I have been called Ada Powell, though by few, and not for some time. May I ask how you have come to know this name?"

He made no attempt to answer her question, his expression breaking into a wide crooked smile that made him appear several years younger. "Miss Powell," he said, leaning forward to rest his arms on the table between them. "I'm glad to make your acquaintance at last. I am hoping you might help me solve a very old mystery."

Relieved by his response, Ada returned his smile. For many years she had been in the business of solving very old mysteries and for a moment she allowed herself to consider that Mr. Allen's arrival at her door did not portend some terrible danger.

"You certainly have my attention, Mr. Allen. How is it you think I may be able to help?"

He sat back in his chair, plunging his right hand into the pocket of his coat and drawing out a tattered book. "I wonder if you've ever read this." He slid it across the table.

Ada coughed into the back of her hand before reaching for the well-worn book. She ran her thumb over the gold letters on the cover: *The Book of Mormon: An Account Written by the Hand of Mormon Upon Plates Taken from the Plates of Nephi*. Missionaries were a common nuisance around the Seaport, but none had ever dared intrude upon Ada's business. A wave of anger washed over her. She pushed the book toward him. "I'm not interested, Mr. Allen."

"Oh, no, no. I gave you the wrong impression, but I'm glad to know you are familiar with the work. I wonder also if you have read this one." From his left pocket he took a second slim book and handed it to her.

"*Mormonism Unvailed* by Eber D. Howe." While Ada read, a shiver traveled down her spine. She knew the book well, but that someone might connect her with it was an uncomfortable notion.

"So, you are not a missionary, then?"

Mr. Allen sighed, sitting straighter in his seat. "Once. Now I am an apostate."

"Lucky for me, but I don't understand. What exactly is this mystery of yours?"

"No doubt you have heard of the many legal entanglements and alleged violence of the Mormon sect in the Utah Territory over the last many years."

Ada nodded. She had read the accounts of the tragedy at Mountain Meadows where a large wagon party made up of Arkansas farmers and their families fell under attack on its way through the Utah Territory. Initially blamed on unfriendly Indians, violent details soon emerged that placed the blame squarely on the shoulders of the Mormons. There were other rumors as well. Stories of apostates murdered as atonement for their sin of attempting to leave the church, of a greedy prophet who forced young girls into illegal marriages, and of a territorial government run on corruption.

"I was a devoted member of the Latter Day Saints as established by the prophet Joseph Smith, but I found I could no longer support a faith built on deceit and brutality. I guess you could say I've been on something of a quest."

"And your quest brought you here? I think you've been misled, Mr. Allen. I know little of Brigham Young's church, only what is reported in the papers."

"Perhaps not, but I've heard you have a gift for finding things that remain hidden from others." Mr. Allen tapped a finger on the cover of Howe's book that now lay closed in front of Ada. "You see, this book describes evidence that might finally cause this whole false religion to crumble. The evidence has been lost for years, though there are those who have attempted to find it."

"And what exactly is this evidence?" Ada wanted to trust this man. He seemed at once so vulnerable and yet self-assured, much like Ada herself. She was drawn to him in that way she always felt drawn to those who sought truth within faith.

"There is a novel, written many years ago by a preacher named Solomon Spalding. The book was not published in his lifetime, but was known to many of his acquaintances, as it was his habit to read aloud long passages from it."

"*Manuscript Found*," Ada whispered before deciding she shouldn't. Mr. Allen's troubled eyes widened with enthusiasm.

"Yes, yes!" he cried, beginning to stand. Seeing that Ada maintained her calm demeanor, Mr. Allen regained his composure and lowered himself once again into his chair. "There are many who have said that it is the true source of *The Book of Mormon*, that the prophet plagiarized the work and claimed it as Divine revelation. I've been looking for it."

"And you believe I can help?"

Mr. Allen shifted in his seat. Ada feared he would stand again and begin pounding on the table as a fiery end-of-days preacher might strike a pulpit. He restrained himself, but it was with new vigor he brought several loose papers from his coat pocket. Mr. Allen shuffled the pages, crumpled and covered in scrawled notes, clearly familiar enough with their contents and organization to know where to find what he needed.

"Ah, my dear Miss Powell, I fear you may be the only one who can help. According to Mr. Howe's book, the many works of Solomon Spalding were stored in a trunk by his widow Mrs. Matilda Davis, but when she allowed Mr. Howe access to them, he found the trunk which should have contained multiple stories contained only one."

"So you believe *Manuscript Found* was removed from the trunk before that time?"

"I do."

"By the widow?"

Mr. Allen shook his head. "I should think she'd stand to gain more from the fame that would accompany revealing the treachery of Joseph Smith than she would from hiding his dirty secret for him. No, I think someone else removed the manuscript, someone who would have had access, but would have attracted little notice."

"And you have some idea of who that might have been?"

"I was hoping that's what you could tell me, Miss Powell."

About the Author

Sarah Angleton is a storyteller and history buff who has degrees in both zoology and literature and still isn't quite sure what she wants to be when she grows up. A Midwestern girl at heart, she spent a brief time living and writing in the beautiful Pacific Northwest before settling near St. Louis where she currently resides with her husband, two sons, and a very loyal dog. Her first work of historical fiction will be available soon from High Hill Press. Find her online at www.Sarah-Angleton.com.

Made in the USA
Columbia, SC
06 February 2020